THE
Faith
RESPONSE

The Faith RESPONSE

Understanding and Applying a
Biblical View of Dependence on God

JOHN R. VAN GELDEREN

CLC
PUBLICATIONS
Fort Washington, PA 19034

The Faith Response
Understanding and Applying a Biblical View of Dependence on God
John R. Van Gelderen

Published by CLC Publications

U.S.A.
P.O. Box 1449, Fort Washington, PA 19034

GREAT BRITAIN
51 The Dean, Alresford, Hants SO24 9BJ

AUSTRALIA
P.O. Box 469, Kippa-Ring QLD 4021

NEW ZEALAND
118 King Street, Palmerston North 4410

Printed in the United States of America
First printing July, 2011

ISBN-10: 1-936143-18-6
ISBN-13: 978-1-936143-18-4

Unless otherwise noted, Scripture quotations are from the Holy Bible, King James Version.
Italicized words in Scripture quotes are the emphasis of the author.

Contents

Preface

Your view of faith affects—well, everything. Since faith is the God-ordained link between your need and God's provision, you must comprehend what faith is and how faith operates. In other words, you must understand the "nuts and bolts" of the faith-life. If wrong ideas regarding faith are woven into the fabric of how you think, then you are hindered greatly in experiencing the life of faith and, consequently, growth in grace.

The Faith Response seeks to unfold God's plan for His children to cooperate with His Word and His Spirit. May the Lord use His truth to bring many into the reality of being "full of faith."

John R. Van Gelderen
June, 2011

Chapter One

The Response of Faith

For it is God which worketh in you both to will and to do of his good pleasure.

Philippians 2:13

Looking unto Jesus, the author and finisher of our faith.

Hebrews 12:2

Faith that moves mountains—is there such a reality? Charlie Kittrell, now with the Lord, would have answered with a resounding "Oh, absolutely!" Charlie served as a pastor for over forty years in Indianapolis, Indiana. Through years of living by faith, he became a man who believed God for a multitude of modern-day miracles.

On one occasion a group of construction workers had just poured fresh cement for the new church building when they noticed a dark line of clouds rapidly moving their way. The imminent and ominous heavy rain threatened to deluge the new cement in a matter of minutes. Pastor Kittrell asked the construction workers what would happen if heavy rain were to hit the fresh cement. They told him it would dimple the cement and ruin it.

He slipped away quickly and quietly to talk to the Lord about the situation. Soon he returned and announced that God was not going to let it rain on the fresh cement. The workers laughed, pointing out that the line of rain clouds was right in front of them and the rain was inevitable.

When anyone challenged God in front of Charlie Kittrell, he would surge within his soul, saying, "God, You must vindicate Yourself," and he cried out in his heart, "Lord do it!" The wall of rain came right up to their church property line and stopped. Not one drop of rain hit the fresh cement.

I personally heard Pastor Kittrell tell this story, and on another occasion I heard another eyewitness verify it. Is not God glorified by such a miracle? Truly, faith moves mountains—and storm clouds!

But what is faith? How does faith operate?

We will seek to answer these two questions later, but for now let's focus on a third question, prompted by the title of this book: What is meant by "the faith response"?

Philippines 2:13 claims, "For it is God which worketh in you both to will and to do of his good pleasure." Hebrews 12:2 affirms, "Looking unto Jesus, the author and finisher of our faith." These biblical statements reveal a *divine order* that must be followed in the life of faith: divine initiation, human responsibility and divine enabling.

Divine Initiation

All good originates with God. Because Adam and Eve sinned in the Garden of Eden, we are a fallen race. Apart from God man is corrupt. Romans 3:10-12 describes our depraved condition: "There is *none righteous, no, not one*: There is none that understandeth, there is *none that seeketh after God.* They are all gone out of the way, they are altogether become unprofitable; there is *none that doeth good, no, not one.*" Without God taking the initiative, no one would ever seek after God on his own. This is true, not only in salvation, but also in sanctification and service. Faith is man's response to God's divine initiation.

Some think that man can just believe—when he desires. This is the misconception of "unfettered choice." But this ignores the reality that "no man can say that Jesus is Lord, but by the Holy Ghost" (1 Cor. 12:13). Without the convicting, convincing work of the Holy Spirit, no one will make a right choice. It will either be the evil works of unrighteousness or the dead works of self-righteousness.

Romans 10:17 states, "So then faith cometh by hearing, and hearing by the word of God." Yet First Corinthians 2:14 states, "But the natural man receiveth not the things of the Spirit of God . . . because they are spiritually discerned." How will man in his depravity exercise "faith . . . by the word of God" if he is a "natural man" that "receiveth not the things of the Spirit of God"? Jesus explains in John 16:8, "He [the Holy Spirit] will reprove [convict, convince] the world of sin, and of righteousness, and of judgment." Faith comes through the Word and the Spirit—it is the Spirit of truth convincing people of the Word of truth. In salvation the Spirit convinces "the world" that "sin" is the problem, "judgment" is the consequence and the "righteousness" of Jesus is the answer, all according to the Word of God.

This same divine order is true in the Christian walk. The Holy Spirit must illumine truth to you and convince you of that truth in order for you to walk by faith. The life of faith is only possible because the indwelling Spirit is faithfully at work in the life of the believer.

In my earliest years of ministry, I thought that since the Word of God makes man responsible to believe, that man could just believe when he wanted to make the choice. Then in 1991 the Lord graciously brought Philippians 2:13 home to my heart through reading Andrew Murray's *Absolute Surrender*, "For it is God which worketh in you . . . to will." I realized that no one would ever make a right choice without the Lord first working in his heart. This was a great awakening to life-shaping truth.

Faith demands divine initiation, but that does not make faith automatic or inevitable. As Jesus said, "No man can come to me, except the Father . . . draw him" (John 6:44). No one comes to Jesus in faith unless he is first "drawn," but man must "come."

Human Responsibility

As clearly as God must first "work" by convincing man of truth, so just as clearly man must then "will" correctly. Jesus is "the author . . . *of our faith*" or, more literally, "the faith of us." God is not the one depending, man is. Yet faith is God-centered because the object of faith is God. Man is always the subject, and God is always the object, of biblical faith.

Man's responsibility is the choice of faith. This is human responsibility or "response-ability." Yet this "response-ability" is not a work. Romans 4:5 articulates, "But to him that worketh not, but believeth on him . . . " Believing, or faith, is the antithesis of human working as this biblical statement makes unquestionably clear. Ephesians 2:8–9 states, "For by grace are ye saved through faith; and that not of yourselves: it is the gift of God: Not of works, lest any man should boast." The way of "faith" is "not of works." Salvation is "by grace" received "through faith." A gift is not earned or purchased by the recipient—a gift is received. The concept of "receiving" in receiving by faith "the gift of God" is not a work. Again, faith is the opposite of works.

Some attempt to argue for the "gift" of faith, in addition to the "gift" of grace. However, care must be taken with this terminology not to confuse or diminish real responsibility. While it is most certainly true that without divine conviction man is not willing to trust in God, it is most certainly *not* true that divine conviction makes faith inevitable.

The issue is man's will. Without divine conviction, man is unwilling to believe in God. But unwillingness is not the same as inability. The fact that the Holy Spirit "convinces" the world of sin, righteousness and judgment (John 16:8) shows that the issue is a will that needs to be convinced. Again, the issue is not inability to believe but unwillingness to believe.

Before certain scriptural passages indicate that certain people *could not* believe, the passages make clear in the context that they first *would not* believe. For example, John 12:37–41 says:

> But though he had done so many miracles before them, yet *they believed not* on him: That the saying of Esaias the prophet might be fulfilled, which he spake, Lord, *who hath believed our report?* and to whom hath the arm of

the Lord been revealed? *Therefore they could not believe,* because that Esaias said again, He hath blinded their eyes, and hardened their heart; that they should not see with their eyes, nor understand with their heart, and be converted, and I should heal them. These things said Esaias, when he saw his glory, and spake of him.

Notice they would not believe ("they believed not . . . who hath believed our report?") before it says, "Therefore they could not believe." This explains the Old Testament quote from Isaiah 6:9–10 as well as parallel passages in the Synoptics.

For example, Matthew 13:14 speaks of those who "seeing ye shall see, and shall not perceive." But the next verse explains why: "their eyes *they* have closed." Ezekiel 12:2 says, "Son of man, thou dwellest in the midst of a rebellious house, which have eyes to see, and see not; they have ears to hear, and hear not: for they are a rebellious house." Again, the issue is "rebellion" or unwillingness, not inability. Matthew 23:37 makes this abundantly clear when Jesus lamented, "O Jerusalem, Jerusalem, thou that killest the prophets, and stonest them which are sent unto thee, how often *would I* have gathered thy children together, even as a hen gathereth her chickens under her wings, and *ye would not!*" Notice Jesus said "would I have" but "ye would not." The issue is unwillingness, not inability. The key is remembering that the ability to believe is not a work: "But to him that worketh not, but believeth . . ."(Rom. 4:5). Faith is not a work; it is dependence upon the Worker—God.

Since the issue is unwillingness, Holy Spirit conviction is needed. But divine conviction can be rejected. Stephen's audience of Jewish leaders in Acts 7 experienced divine conviction of truth so powerfully that "they were cut to the heart" (7:54). But Stephen said plainly, "Ye do always resist the Holy Ghost" (7:51). They resisted Holy Spirit conviction. Some argue that if man can resist God, that it makes God less than God. But this ignores the explicit statement that the Jewish leaders resisted the Holy Spirit—a statement which is divinely inspired. Also, this ignores the possibility that God, in His sovereign wisdom, might choose to make man truly responsible for his choices. This does not diminish God's sovereignty.

Divine conviction does not make faith inevitable. As "unfettered choice" is a misconception that ignores the necessity for divine conviction, so "inevitable faith" is a misconception that ignores real human responsibility. Returning to the terminology of "the gift of faith," it must be remembered that "the gift of faith" is not a "given." Faith must not be thought of as an outside foreign element entered into man. This would make faith inevitable. Rather, the gift of faith comes by way of divine conviction, without which faith would not be exercised. But divine conviction can be received or resisted.

By way of analogy, suppose you get quite sick. Then a friend convinces you that a particular physician can truly help you. In fact, you are so convinced that you entrust yourself to that doctor's care. In a sense, your friend gave you "the gift of faith" in that physician. But you could have chosen to reject your friend's convincing words. Similarly, when the Holy Spirit convinces you to trust in God, and you respond in faith, there is a sense in which the Spirit gave you "the gift of faith," but only in that sense. That gift could have been rejected.

Faith is neither an unfettered choice nor an inevitable choice. Faith is a responsible choice—a response of God-dependence because of divine conviction. Faith is that for which man is responsible, but faith is not a work. In fact, faith is the only responsibility for which God holds man accountable—faith to receive the eternal life of Jesus in salvation and faith to access the abundant life of Jesus in sanctification and service. The former is faith for a new standing. The latter is faith for a new walking. But faith is that for which God holds man responsible. The only thing we as humans can "do" is to admit that we cannot do anything—only God can—so we must put our trust in God step by step, from beginning to end.

Some argue that a faith emphasis in theology is human-centered and could give man the right to boast. But that reveals a lack of understanding of the nature of faith, which is true God-dependence. How can this be human-centered? What is there to boast about? "Where is boasting then? It is excluded. By what law? of works? Nay: but by the law of faith" (Rom. 3:27). This passage explicitly says that "the law of faith" excludes boasting, because it realizes, "I can't, but God can." Faith, if it boasts in anything, boasts in God. Faith is not a work; it is dependence on the Worker. All the glory goes to God.

Since faith is not a work, it does not violate the principle that all we have is by God's grace. Through faith we are saved by grace (Eph. 2:8) and by faith we have access to grace to stand firm in our Christian walk (Rom. 5:2). But since faith is not a work, it never diminishes grace. Obviously what you believe regarding the role of faith in salvation greatly affects what you believe regarding its role in sanctification.

Some of the early leaders of the Reformation saw the light of justification by grace through faith, and rightly concluded that salvation is not by works. But others, by making the false assumption that faith is a work, were led to the equally false conclusion that regeneration must *precede* faith if justification is not of works. This misconception was the root of a misguided theology that applies intellectual gymnastics to many passages in an attempt to reconcile it to Scripture.

God makes it plain that faith is not a human "work." The verse "But to him that worketh not, but believeth on him . . ." (Rom. 4:5) leaves us no room to think otherwise. There have been many major theological battles over this issue, so we need to keep our view of faith in a biblical balance between extremes. Faith is neither an unfettered choice nor an inevitable choice, but a responsible choice. The divine order regarding faith begins with divine initiation followed by human responsibility. Then God enables.

Divine Enabling

Philippians 2:13 says, "For it is God which worketh in you both to will *and to do of his good pleasure.*" Hebrews 12:2 affirms, "Looking unto Jesus, the author *and finisher* of our faith." God responds to those who respond to Him. When man believes in Christ as Savior, he is regenerated and much more (John 3:16, 18, 36; 5:24; 6:47). When man takes a step of faith, God enables according to the step of faith taken (Col. 2:6; Rom. 5:2). Faith (God-dependence) accesses grace (Spirit-enabling) to think right, speak right, do right and so forth. The walk of faith accesses growth in grace. Jesus said, "Abide in me [faith], and I in you [grace] . . . for without me ye can do nothing" (John 15:4–5). But with Him, you can do everything He leads you to do—through divine enabling.

Recently I witnessed to a young unsaved mother. At the beginning of the conversation, she was not even sure that God existed. The Lord led me to patiently walk her down a thorough pathway of salvation truth. Throughout this journey, the Holy Spirit did His convincing work that sin is the problem, hell is the consequence, and Christ alone is the answer. This constituted divine initiation. Then she bowed her head and expressed faith in Christ as her Savior. This constituted human responsibility. Of course, the Lord is always true to His Word and regenerated her. This constituted divine enabling. She was born again! In fact, she even gave testimony to this the next Lord's Day at a Bible-believing church.

This is God's divine order regarding faith—divine initiation, human responsibility and divine enabling. What is true in faith for salvation is also true for every step of faith, whether it be for victorious living or effective serving. The order is the same. We must follow the divine order in the life of faith and learn to respond to God that He might respond to our faith in Him. This is *responsible faith*.

Chapter Two

The Concept of Faith

Now faith is the substance of things hoped for, the evidence of things not seen. . . . But without faith it is impossible to please him: for he that cometh to God must believe that he is, and that he is a rewarder of them that diligently seek him.
Hebrews 11:1, 6

So then faith cometh by hearing, and hearing by the word of God.

Romans 10:17

Well do I remember getting into the car of a faculty member at my college who sold quality diamonds to students for reasonable prices. As soon as I got into the car, he unveiled a breathtaking gem. I sat there stunned. The beauty of this diamond flashed with each twist as the sunlight reflected a new facet of beauty to my eye. Sold!

This stone was set in the engagement ring I would give to Mary Lynn, the love of my life. Later, in a scenic setting by a pond in the woods, after accepting my proposal for marriage, I revealed the diamond ring to Mary Lynn. As she gazed at the beautiful diamond, it was apparent that she was truly pleased.

Isn't it amazing that something as simple as a diamond— a piece of crystallized carbon—is so highly treasured? And though simple, a diamond has many facets. From God's perspective, faith is like a diamond. Without it, it is impossible to please God.

The Many Facets of Faith

Faith, though simple in its essence, is multifaceted in nature. Do we understand its many facets, or have erroneous ideas regarding faith somehow been woven into the fabric of our thinking? We will be greatly hindered in the life of faith unless we keep before us six scriptural facets of this priceless diamond.

Facet 1: The essence of faith is dependence

Any simple definition of the noun *faith* leads to words such as "trust," "reliance" or "dependence," and of the verb *believe* to phrases such as "to trust in," "to rely on" and "to depend on." The concept of *dependence* incorporates the entire soul of a human being—mind, affections and will. All three agents of the soul must be involved in order "to depend on."

Although biblical faith involves dependence in the realm of the unseen, for the moment consider it in the visible realm. When you sit on a chair, you exercise faith or dependence in that chair. First, in your mind you understand that the object before you is a chair. Next, in your affections what you understand "affects" you: as you agree that the chair can hold your weight, you have the desire to sit down. Finally, in your will you decide to depend on the chair by actually sitting down and placing your weight on that chair. To stand there and say, "I believe that chair can hold my weight" but never sit down in the chair would be "easy-believism" in the chair. It would constitute believing *about* the chair without believing *in* the chair. This would be acknowledging that the chair could hold your weight but never depending on the chair to hold your weight.

But faith is not merely acknowledging—faith is depending. Faith believes not merely *about*, but believes *on*. The first facet in forming a definition of faith is that the essence of faith is dependence. Our definition for faith thus far consists of one word: *dependence*.

Facet 2: The object of biblical faith is God

Leaving the visible realm, we enter the realm of biblical faith—dependence on God Himself: "But without faith it is impossible to please him: for he that cometh *to God* must believe that he is, and that he is a rewarder of them that diligently seek him" (Heb. 11:6). Throughout this verse the focus is not the subject of faith (you), but the object of faith (God). What a blessing and relief! The key is not us, but God. If you want more faith, get to know God better, for He is the object of faith.

Why then does it say in First John 5:4 "and this is the victory that overcometh the world, even our faith"? Isn't Christ the victory? How then can *faith* be the victory? The answer lies in the fact that faith is not a work; it is dependence on the Worker—who is the victory. Faith then brings you into union with God, who is the victory.

In Luke 17:11–18 Jesus healed ten lepers, but only one returned to thank Him. In verse 19 Jesus said to the one who returned, "Arise, go thy way: *thy faith hath made thee whole*" (something He often said to those he healed). On the surface this may seem contradictory, but faith is not a work; it is dependence on the Worker. Faith made the leper whole by simply bringing him into union with Christ, the Healer.

As an evangelist, I bring my family along on many of my trips in a recreational vehicle. When my son was two or three years old, he couldn't negotiate the steps when leaving the trailer, so I would go ahead of him and take the steps down to the ground. Then turning to him I would say, "Come on, John," and he would jump from the top step into my arms. If I did not catch him, he would have hit the pavement. It was a leap of dependence—of faith—on his part, and his dependence brought him into union with me as I caught him in my arms. Likewise faith brings us into union with the strong object of our faith—God Himself, where "underneath are the everlasting arms" (Deut. 33:27).

By combining the first two facets we have a two-word definition of faith: *God-dependence.* But what is the basis for dependence on God? This leads us to view a third facet on the diamond of faith.

Facet 3: *The basis of faith in God is the Word of God*

On what foundation is dependence on God based? The answer is clear in Romans 10:17: "So then faith cometh by hearing, and hearing by *the word* of God." The basis for depending on God is the Word of God. Interestingly, John 1:1 and 1:14 teach that Jesus Christ is "the Word." There is a mystery of oneness between the inscribed Word and the incarnate Word, between the written Word and the living Word.

We would know only general information about God from what is revealed in nature—what Paul refers to as "his eternal power and Godhead" (Rom. 1:20)—apart from the specific revelation of the Word of God. That Word is the basis for our depending upon God. In other words, the food of faith is the Word of God. If you desire to live more by faith, you must feed on the Word of the living God. This third defining facet allows us to now expand our definition of faith into a phrase: *God-dependence based on God's Word.*

Facet 4: *The foundation of the Word of God is specific, not general*

When Romans 10:17 states, "So then faith cometh by hearing, and hearing by *the word* of God," it is significant to note the Greek word translated "word." When referring to the Scriptures, there are two words that are translated as "word" in the English Bible. The word *logos* is the larger, more general term and often refers to the entire Word of God. For example, when Jesus stated, "Thy word is truth" (John 17:17), He used the word *logos*, clearly indicating that the entire Word of God is truth.

The other word, *rhema*, is the smaller, more specific term, referring to a part of the larger whole—a single word, a phrase, a sentence, a paragraph or a section of scriptural text. A *rhema* is a specific reference within the larger *logos*—a specific slice of the whole pie.

Which word do you think is incorporated in Romans 10:17 ("faith" comes "by the *word* of God")? When speaking on this verse, I often ask this question of my audience, and the most common answer they give is *logos,* because the whole of Scripture is the foundation for our faith. While that is most certainly true, amazingly Romans 10:17 uses the word *rhema.*

The significance of this can be literally life-changing. The foundation for faith is specific, not general. The basis for trusting God is because God specifically gives His word regarding a given matter. In salvation someone must have the specific words of the gospel message. It may be John 3:16 or perhaps the "Romans Road." But specific salvation truth must be grasped in order for one to trust in Christ as their Savior. The same is true for walking by faith. Even if you are depending on the character of God regarding a matter, we know of His character through the words of God that reveal His character.

God-dependence comes by communication, and communication by the Word of God—the specific word of God. Or we might say that faith comes by the words of God—the "exceeding great and precious promises" (2 Pet. 1:4). Therefore, as we turn the diamond of faith allowing the defining facet of the *rhema* to shine, our definition of faith may now be adjusted by changing "God's Word" to "God's words": *God-dependence based on God's words.* But there is another important facet to consider.

Facet 5: The specific foundation is real, though not in the sensory realm

Hebrews 11:1 says, "Now faith is the *substance* [substantive, real, reality] of things hoped for, the evidence of things *not seen.*" The dependence of biblical faith unites with that which is real, though not seen (and, by implication, not felt emotionally). In other words, biblical faith is not in the physical realm of the senses or the emotional realm of the soul. The specific foundation for faith, the *rhema* of the words of God, is real, though "not seen." Faith deals with invisible realities.

But this is contrary to human nature; we tend to believe only what we can see and feel. Even some of God's people who intellectually know that "we walk by faith, not by sight" (2 Cor. 5:7) still look for a visible encouragement to their faith. It is easy to pray for the sick to be healed when they still look good. But what if they don't? Faith must go beyond the sensory realm to discerning the mind of the Lord on a given matter. If your "faith" depends on what you see, you do not have biblical faith at all. Biblical faith penetrates deeper than the sensory realm and "sees" the unseen realities that inspire hope. I fear that there is so much unbelief woven into our thinking patterns that depending on the reality of the unseen may seem totally foreign to the present-day saint.

Implicitly, not only is the specific foundation for faith not seen, it is also not felt. In other words, faith is not a feeling. Yet many of God's children seek a feeling that they equate with faith.

I was born in the old cowboy town of Durango located on the western slope of the Rocky Mountains in southwest Colorado. When I was born in 1962, Durango was still a genuine cowboy town. But when I was four years of age, we moved from there to the city limits of the south side of Chicago. This, of course, constituted a radical change. We lived several years in the city limits and then moved to the suburbs where I spent the rest of my boyhood and teenage years. As a result, I am not a cowboy; I am a "city-slicker."

However, in the nineties my wife and I were in a revival meeting in the Durango church my father used to pastor. While there, some older family friends who owned a three-thousand acre ranch invited me to go horseback riding. I had seen horses before—I had even sat on the back of a horse—but as a city kid, I knew nothing about riding one "out on the range." So, excited about the opportunity, I said I would go. But down deep I was a bit uneasy, knowing this was out of my comfort zone.

The day we went riding was comfortably cool, with a deep blue sky. Three of us were in the party, the head cowboy of that ranch, another westerner and me. They showed me many beautiful views that the acreage offered. At one point we saw in the distance a breath-taking view of the majestic, snow-covered La Plata Mountains in the San Juan Range.

Eventually we came to a spot where a narrow ledge went around the curvature of the mountainside. The next thing I knew, the lead cowboy took his horse right out on that ledge, which meant we followed. Suddenly I was very aware of my environment. To my left I could see the mountain wall as it continued to rise upward, and I could almost reach out and touch it. That was somewhat comforting. To my right I could see nothing unless I looked down, and it was a long way down a steep slope, ending with a mountain stream with big boulders. That was *not* comforting. Yet somehow we made it past that precarious spot.

Later we came to an area where not only could you look to the right and see nothing unless you looked down, you could look to the left and see nothing unless you looked down. We were riding along a ridge. Again, this new turf unnerved my city-upbringing.

But then we came to a spot where it was still extremely steep to the right. To my shock, the lead cowboy moved his reins to the right and started taking his horse straight down that steep slope. It was so steep that the hind legs of his horse basically tucked up under, and the horse skidded its way down, dislodging rocks as it went along. While watching in utter amazement, I thought to myself, "That guy is crazy!"

The next cowboy, as if there was nothing to it, moved his reins to the right and also began taking his horse straight down the same steep slope. The hind legs of his horse tucked up under and began to skid downward as well.

Obviously, I was supposed to follow. But there was one old cowboy word that I remembered, and I yelled it out for all it was worth: *Whoa*! Thankfully, the well-trained horse stopped immediately. When I yelled out, the cowboy skidding down the slope below me looked up and said, perplexingly, "John, what's wrong?" I do not remember what I said, but I obviously revealed that I was petrified. Although he could have had a little fun in the situation, he graciously instructed, "Just loosen up on the reins, and the horse will take you down." But that was exactly what I was afraid of!

Finally I loosened up on the reigns, and I *depended* on that horse to take me down the slope, which it safely did. However, I must hasten to explain that while I was in the process of depending on the horse, my feelings were not in line with my dependence!

We could describe this as "clinging faith." In fact, I was hanging on for dear life. However, in contrast, we could describe the other cowboys as demonstrating a "resting faith." Clinging faith describes dependence that is contrary to your emotions. Resting faith describes dependence that is amenable to your emotions. It is not a matter of two kinds of faith. Dependence is dependence. It is a matter of two *positions* of dependence: one *clinging* and the other *resting*.

You have to be in the position of resting faith in order to be able to help others, just as that cowboy helped me. But how do you transition from clinging faith to resting faith? The answer is found in the progression of truth in Romans 5:2–5. Clinging faith is seen in the phrase "tribulation worketh patience"; the confident expectation of resting faith is seen in the word "hope." The key to transitioning from clinging faith to resting faith is seen in the word that lies between: *experience.*

By the time my horse and I got to the bottom of that steep slope, I had some experience under my belt, and the thought crossed my mind, "That wasn't so bad. I could do that again." Of course, I *didn't* do it again, but the thought at least crossed my mind.

There may be some areas where you have trusted God repeatedly and have come to a resting faith for that issue. Other areas may take you out of your comfort zone, and you must exercise clinging faith, but through experience you may move to a resting faith.

Some writers of the past used an illustration known as "Mr. Fact, Mr. Faith and Mr. Feeling." As long as Mr. Faith focuses on Mr. Fact, eventually Mr. Feeling will come along. But if Mr. Faith focuses on Mr. Feeling, enamored by the "warm and fuzzy" flutters, he loses sight of Mr. Fact and crumbles altogether.

We must keep looking unto Jesus by focusing on the facts of God's words regardless of feelings. Faith is not a feeling. This must be remembered when you step out of your comfort zone, whether it be when handing out a gospel tract, declaring the gospel, child-training, apologizing or some other issue.

The specific foundation of the *rhema* of God is real, though this "realness" is not in the sensory realm. Our definition may now be expanded with this added facet: *God-dependence based on the reality of God's words* (regardless of what you see and feel). This leads us to one more defining facet of faith.

Facet 6: It is the Spirit who convinces us of the reality of the Word

How can you depend on the reality of what you cannot see or feel? You must be convinced of its reality. You need evidence of the reality of the non-sensory realm. Hebrews 11:1 says, "Now faith is the substance [reality] of things hoped for, the *evidence* of things not seen." This word *evidence*, meaning proof, occurs as a noun in only one other text of Scripture: "All scripture is given by inspiration of God, and is profitable for doctrine, for *reproof* . . ." (2 Tim. 3:16). The same word translated *reproof* here is translated *evidence* in Hebrews 11:1.

When I first noticed this, I wondered what the connection was between *evidence* and *reproof*. This became clear when I looked at the verb form, *reprove*, in John 16:8: ". . . he [the Holy Spirit] will *reprove* the world of sin, and of righteousness and of judgment." The word *reprove* means to convict or convince someone of something, and *evidence* is the proof used to convict or convince someone.

Who is the convincer? The Holy Spirit is the one who convinces of the grand realities of truth connected to the

words of God, which form the specific foundational stepping stones on the pathway of faith. When the Holy Spirit
illumines scriptural truth, that illumination brings conviction—that is *evidence.* It is the Word made convincing by
the Spirit. In a certain sense it is an encounter with God.
This is what is needed to depend on the reality of what you
cannot see or feel.

As you listen to a preacher unfold a particular passage,
or you study and meditate on that passage privately, and the
light begins to dawn on the horizon of that passage (either
slowly or suddenly), that is Holy Spirit illumination. The
Spirit convinces you of the truth of that specific passage. This
conviction provides the evidence needed to exercise faith.
When God blesses you in this way, don't just say to yourself,
"That was nice; I got stirred." Instead, recognize that God is
giving you evidence—and He knows that, sooner than you
may think, you are going to need it.

Faith is not wishful thinking. It is convinced confidence
through the Word and the Spirit. As the Spirit convinces
you of unseen scriptural realities, He is revealing to you the
Father's will and offering you His power to follow His will.
Faith, then, unites with God's will and power.

By incorporating all six facets of the diamond of faith that
have shined on our understanding, we may complete our definition of faith: *God-dependence based on Spirit-conviction of
the reality of God's words.* Faith is the simple choice to depend
on the reality of the words of God because the Spirit of God
has convinced you of that reality regardless of what you may
see or feel. Faith then unites with God's will and God's power
through God's Word and God's Spirit. Faith is the simple key
that unlocks the storehouse of God's provision.

An Example of Faith

Since "without faith it is impossible to please him," we must learn the biblical concept of faith in order to live a life of faith that truly pleases God. As we have seen, faith may be likened to a diamond in the sense that it is simple in its essence, yet multifaceted in its nature. But faith is not like a diamond in the sense that faith is not a work, nor is it the expression of work as in the purchase of a diamond. Yet faith pleases God. When we apply God-dependence based on Spirit-conviction of the reality of God's words, God says that He is pleased.

Some of my dear friends in Myanmar (formerly called Burma) exemplify God-pleasing faith. Timothy and Lily regularly demonstrate walking by faith. When obstacles arise that seem to block their path ahead, they simply pray—and watch God work. For them this is normal living.

Once while I was there preaching in a conference of over 1,200 people, 103 of whom had walked for three days to attend, a decision had to be made as to our departure time. Smoke from burning trees in the nearby mountains had obscured the airport runway and had already delayed our arrival by causing us to travel via car instead of plane. But the smoke still lingered over the valley. We had already missed some of the conference because of arriving late. To leave early to travel to Mandalay by car would cause us to miss even more of the conference. Yet if the smoke remained, our flight would not be able to land in order to fly us out in time to catch our U.S. flights from Yangon.

So Timothy, Lily and others sought the face of God. Later Timothy announced that they were going to have us stay to the end of the conference, that the smoke would be cleared, that the plane would arrive on time and that we would leave at the scheduled time. In order to facilitate this, they prayed that God would send rain to clear away the smoke, even though it had not rained for several months and was not "supposed" to rain for a while because it was not their rainy season.

On the last day of the conference, the thunder rolled as lightning lit up the skies, and rain poured down long enough to clear away the lingering smoke. The next day our plane arrived, and we left at the scheduled time.

This faith—simple faith in God—undoubtedly pleased the Lord. In upcoming chapters we will discuss how faith like this operates. But for now the point is that this was faith—and God was pleased.

Chapter Three

The Exercise of Faith: Possessing Facts

Every place that the sole of your foot shall tread upon, that have I given unto you.

Joshua 1:3

For we walk by faith.

2 Corinthians 5:7

Israel's conquest of Canaan in the book of Joshua is a beautiful illustration of the believer taking possession of all that is his in Christ. As one writer explains:

> Before they crossed the Jordan, they had a declaration from God that every place that the sole of their feet should tread upon HAD BEEN GIVEN THEM; but they had to walk over it, and take it foot by foot—for God did not hand it over to them and say, "Now you have it," so that they had nothing further to do. He said, "I *have* given it. Now *you* must take it step by step."[1]

33

The children of Israel had been given possessions. But they had the responsibility of *possessing* their possessions. The concept of possessing is inherent in the phrase "Every place that the sole of your foot shall tread upon"; the concept of possessions is inherent in the phrase "that have I given unto you." They had to exercise faith step by step to possess their possessions. The same is true for the believer and his inheritance in Christ. This concept moves beyond what faith is to how faith operates.

"Walking" by faith demands the "exercise" of faith. The life of faith demands steps of faith—simply taking one step at a time. Consequently, the past and future must not be the concern, but the present step at hand. While these steps may vary according to the need of the moment, the appropriate ones must be taken in order to proceed in the life of faith.

Faith is not passive but active. It is not passively "doing nothing" in the name of trusting; it is actively trusting God to do something. Faith is not merely acknowledging that God can do something; it is depending on God to actually do it. Anything less than that is taking a stance of "easy-believism" regarding sanctification and service. This is the "dead" faith that James warns against (2:14–26). Faith must take steps—not a human work of trying, but a step of trusting God to work. This is the exercise of faith, described scripturally as "the work of faith" (1 Thess. 1:3; 2 Thess. 2:11).

Just as the children of Israel had to exercise faith in order to possess their possessions, so we must dare to possess our possessions in Christ. How? It depends on whether we are exercising faith in the *fact* of a present possession or the *promise* of a future possession.

In school days, did you ever wonder in English class if the points of grammar would make a difference in your life? Amazingly, the point of grammar that distinguishes a fact from a promise can actually make a significant difference in your walk with God. Facts are in the present tense or refer to past events with present ramifications. Promises are in the future tense, either by being stated as such explicitly or by being implied as such because of a condition that must first be met. Facts refer to that which *is*. Promises refer to that which *will be*. Facts represent *realities*. Promises represent "potentialities."

The story is told of a time when G. Campbell Morgan taught a Bible class. After expounding a particular phrase of Scripture, he exclaimed, "Isn't this a wonderful promise?" To his surprise an older lady replied, "No, Mr. Campbell, this is *not* a wonderful promise. It is a precious reality!" This lady understood the difference between the *reality* of what *is* (a fact), versus the *potentiality* of what *will be* (a promise).

Facts are the provision for your immediate or present need. Promises are the provision for your coming or future need. Facts form the foundation of faith for your present experience. Promises form the foundation of faith for your future experience. Yet both facts and promises are glorious possessions that must be possessed. This chapter will focus on possessing facts, the next chapter on possessing promises.

How do you possess facts? Since facts represent the present reality of what is, dare to face the facts of God's provision and claim them as your present experience. Let's consider two major examples of how faith operates in possessing facts.

"Christ in You"

The first major example regards the reality of Christ in the believer. As just noted, to access this provision you must first face the facts and then claim them.

Face the facts (the present reality of what is)

The scriptural statements of fact regarding Christ in the believer are numerous. Galatians 2:20 says, "I am crucified with Christ; nevertheless I live, yet not I but Christ liveth in me." If you are born again, then the moment you believed in Jesus Christ you were separated from indwelling sin (you were crucified/died to sin), and you were joined to the indwelling Christ. Literally, in the spirit part of your being, your unregenerated spirit that was joined to indwelling sin was forever severed from that defiling relationship. Yet you were raised with Christ a new man—regenerated. Your regenerated spirit was then joined to the indwelling Christ so that you were forever sealed to a new purifying relationship.

Indwelling sin still seeks to usurp authority in your life, but it has no authority. You have been separated (died to) indwelling sin. Prior to this liberation, you were forced to serve sin. Now you may serve sin if you so choose, but it is voluntary service.

However, the good news is that your spirit is joined to the Spirit of Christ. As Galatians 2:20 affirms, Christ is living in you. Christ moved into your being to impart to you His victorious life. You have been liberated from a bad master to a good master. This new master does not force service from you, He beseeches you to gladly yield to Him as Lord. Yet when you take His yoke upon you, you will find that it is easy because He Himself carries the weight.

This is the provision of "Christ liveth in me." The verb "liveth" is in the present tense. Christ *is living* in every believer—in you. It is not that Christ *will* live in you, He *is* living in you. This is a matter of actual fact. As Galatians 2:20 further states, this fact must be accessed by faith to fully benefit you. But before you can claim the facts, you must face the facts. You must apprehend the present reality: *Christ is living in you.* Let that truth penetrate the depths of your being.

Colossians 1:27 reiterates this truth with the grand statement "Christ in you, the hope of glory." Colossians 3:4 further declares, "Christ . . . is our life." Philippians 1:21 states, "For to me to live is Christ." Christ is truly living in every believer. Face the facts. Face the reality of what presently *is*: Christ in you!

On this basis Second Corinthians 12:9 claims, "My grace is sufficient for thee." This is a present-tense fact. It is not that His grace *will be* sufficient, His grace *is* sufficient right now because Christ is living in you. Grace is the Spirit of Christ enabling you with the life of Christ.

Discover the secret of *is*. Discover the secret of *Christ in you* as the great "I AM" for all your present needs. The following account beautifully illustrates this discovery in the life of Hanmer Webb-Peploe of England:

> By 1874 he had six children and a small stipend. Fourteen years "a faithful preacher of the doctrine of justification," his existence was a "constant watching, waiting and struggling to do right. . . . I had no joy for every moment, no rest in the midst of trouble, no calm amid the burdens of this life; I was strained and overstrained until I felt I was breaking down."

That year he took his family for a seaside holiday at Saltburn on the Yorkshire coast. Stevenson Blackwood was also on vacation and told him of the Oxford Conference opening that very day: "He said, 'People are coming together there to seek for a blessing, to pray for the life of rest.' He looked me in the face and said, 'Have you rest?'" When Webb-Peploe understood his meaning, he replied, "That is what I long for most." A friend of Blackwood's sent daily reports from Oxford, and they went into the woods and read them together.

Webb-Peploe's six-month-old son Edward Alec died at Saltburn, and he carried the little coffin back alone across England in the train to bury him. His holiday spoiled, his heart sore, an unexpected Sunday ahead in his own church, he tried to prepare a sermon, choosing from the set lesson a text: "My grace is sufficient for thee." He could not concentrate. He resented "all God called upon me to bear. I flung down my pen, threw myself on my knees and said to God 'It is *not* sufficient, it is not sufficient! Lord, *let* Thy grace be sufficient. O Lord, do!'" He opened his eyes and saw on the wall a framed text which his mother had given him the day before he left for holiday and the servant had hung during his absence. In scrolls and squiggles and colored inks it proclaimed: "My grace is sufficient for thee." The word "is" showed up bright green. A voice seemed to say, "You fool, how dare you ask God to make what *is*! Get up and take, and you will find it true. When God says 'is' it is for you to believe Him." Webb-Peploe got up. "That 'is' changed my life. From that moment I could say, 'O God, whatever Thou dost say in Thy Word I believe, and, please God, I will step out upon it.'"

He took God at His word, he believed the *fact*, and his life was revolutionized. He entered into such an experience of rest and peace, such trust in a sufficient Savior, as he never before had dreamed could be possible. Within a month the governess in the family said to Mrs. Webb-Peploe, "The farmers are remarking how much changed the vicar is: he does not seem fretful any more, but seems to be quiet and gentle about everything." And from that day to this, now forty-five years later, many have praised God that the life of this minister of the gospel is a testimony to the sufficiency of the grace which God declares is a fact.[2]

Webb-Peploe dared to face the fact that "My grace is sufficient for thee" and then claimed it as his present experience. The supernatural impact of accessing the present reality of all-sufficient grace transformed his life.

Claim the facts (as your present experience)

Once you face the facts, you must claim them. But how do you lay claim on the reality of what *is*? Simply put, two steps of faith comprise the "claiming."

First, *take* the reality of what has already been provided. Second, *act* upon it. It is not merely acting, for acting without first taking is self-dependence—acting independently of God. It is taking and then acting. This is God-dependence—acting with dependence upon God. Notice there is no need to "ask" for what already is. Actually, asking reveals unbelief in the "presentness" of the fact. "Satan's great device," William Newell wrote, "is to drive earnest souls back to beseeching God for what God says has already been done."[3]

Besides, there is often no time to ask. Just *take* and *act* accordingly.

For example, when faced with that which might tempt you to think impurely, if you already know that Christ is in you and His grace is sufficient, claim the facts with: "Your purity, Lord" (*take*), and look the other way (*act*). As you lay claim on your provision, you will experience a freedom to look the other way by the power of the Holy Spirit and be free from what you saw as if you never saw it. This is a glorious provision.

Or when faced with that which might tempt you to impatience, knowing your provision, claim the facts with: "Your patience, Lord" (*take*), and begin to speak a soft answer, trusting Him to enable you with His patience (*act*). As you lay claim on Christ in you, you will experience His patience to respond rightly to the situation.

Since the gift is not to be separated from the Giver, when you really face the fact of Christ in you, you can claim His life in any circumstance: "Your life, Lord." The key is that you actually *take*. It cannot be a matter of asking "Your life, Lord?" for you do not need to ask for what is. It must be a matter of taking "Your life, Lord."

In fact, if you really are convinced of the present reality of Christ in you, you can simply claim that reality with: "Thank You, Lord, for Your victorious life." Or "Thank You for Your purity." Or "Thank You for Your patience." Or "Thank You for Your love," and so on. Thanking implies that you "took." Once you have discovered the secret of *is* (as a result of which you *take*), you can then discover the secret of saying "Thank You" (because you *took*). Just thank the Lord ("Thank You, Lord, for Your victorious life") to then do what would otherwise be impossible—by His life. This comprises the steps of *taking* and *acting*. This is claiming the facts.

As Charles Trumbull rightly says, "The secret of victory is not praying, but praising; not asking, but thanking. All eternity will not be long enough to finish praising and thanking our Lord Jesus Christ for the simple, glorious fact that His grace IS sufficient for us."[4]

Trumbull continues to explain that Christ *is* living in the believer, not *will be*. God's grace *is* sufficient, not *will be*. These facts are not something God will do if you ask; He is doing it anyway, and therefore, you do not need to ask. But the fact of Christ living in you and the reality of God's grace will not be *manifested* in your life if you do not depend upon the reality of these facts by *taking* what has already been provided, and *acting* upon that provision. Unbelief essentially attempts to make God a liar. Unbelief essentially says that what God declares to be fact is not so. But faith lays hold on the reality of "Christ in you." Faith, therefore, lays hold on the *is* of grace. "The moment we *believe* in this God-declared fact," Trumbull says, "there is a sufficiency of omnipotence successfully at work in our lives that makes us more than conquerors and leads us in triumph."[5]

"You in Christ"

The second major example of how faith operates in possessing facts regards the reality of the believer in Christ. Again, to access this provision you must first face the facts and then claim them.

Face the facts (the present reality of what is)

Ephesians 1:19–21 and 2:6 declares, "And what is the exceeding greatness of his power to us-ward who believe, according to the working of his mighty power, which he wrought in Christ, when he raised him from the dead, and set him at his own right hand in the heavenly places, far above all principality, and power, and might, and dominion, and every name that is named, not only in this world, but also in that which is to come . . . and hath raised us up together, and made us sit together in heavenly places in Christ Jesus."

God displayed His mighty power "when he raised [Christ] from the dead, and set him at his own right hand in the heavenly places, far above all" and when he "raised us up together, and made us sit together in heavenly places in Christ Jesus." What an amazing fact! This is a case of a past event with present ramifications.

At salvation you as a believer were placed into Christ. Christ now sits at the throne in the heavenly or spiritual realm. This throne position represents His authority. Since you are in Christ, you too are at the throne—the position of authority over the Enemy.

The spiritual realm does not know the geographical boundaries of the physical realm. Therefore, although your body is on earth in the physical realm, in the spiritual realm your spirit which is joined to Christ through the Holy Spirit is actually in Christ at the throne. Christ presently sits "far above all principality, and power, and might, and dominion, and every name that is named." As Ruth Paxson so aptly states, "In Christ we are as far above the power of Satan as Christ is."[6] Face the facts. Let the Spirit illumine the present reality of your position in Christ far above the powers of darkness. Apprehend your position in Christ at the throne.

Claim the facts (as your present experience)

Having faced the facts, you may now claim them. Again, two steps of faith comprise the claiming. First, *take* the reality of what is. Second, *act* upon it. For example, when Satan hurls a fiery dart at you, which is a thought injected into your mind with no visible trigger for that thought, simply thank the Lord for your safety at the throne (*take*) and reject the thought (*act*). The moment you do, the evil thought vanishes. This is lifting up the shield of faith by which you may quench all the fiery darts of the wicked one (Eph. 6:16).

If you are in a given thought process, and suddenly, seemingly out of nowhere, evil thoughts roll across your brain (perhaps angry thoughts, impure thoughts or arrogant thoughts), from your heart simply say in confidence, "Thank you, Lord, for my position in Christ at the throne," (*take*) and therefore, "I reject that fiery dart" (*act*). The shield of faith then wielded extinguishes Satan's fiery dart, and you are free. What a glorious possession to be possessed!

When you have a day where there seems to be excessive aggravating circumstances, recognize the excessiveness as a possible mark of Satan's workings. Then stop and claim the facts of your position in Christ over the Enemy. Simply thank the Lord for your position of safety in Him (*take*) and exercise His authority over anything that is from Satan (*act*). As you submit yourself to God (*take*) and resist the devil (*act*), the devil must flee from you (James 4:7).

In all of these applications, Christ won the victory at the cross. Facing the facts and claiming them is simply possessing the ground that Christ already won. But it must be possessed, or you will miss the blessing.

Ruth Paxson, missionary to China, suggests claiming your position in Christ at the throne when you awake each morning. This immediately protects you from the Enemy and opens the way for a blessed time with God. I have applied this truth for years for me and my family, and found it to be a blessing.

The exercise of faith is a matter of possessing your possessions in Christ. This involves possessing facts as well as promises. Dare to face the facts of God's provision and claim them as your present experience. Simply *take* what is, thanking the Lord, and *act* upon it. Christ then is manifested as your present experience. This is how you possess *facts*. In the next chapter we will address how to possess *promises*.

Chapter Four

The Exercise of Faith: Possessing Promises

Who through faith . . . obtained promises.

Hebrews 11:33

While the facts of Scripture are for the here and now, the promises of Scripture are for the days ahead. Just as we need to face the facts of what God declares to *be* and *claim* them as our present experience, we need to face the promises of what God declares *will be* and *obtain* them as our future experience.

The exceedingly great and precious promises of God open a whole new vista of potential for every believer. When the Spirit speaks a promise to the heart of a child of God, He leads that believer to the evidence needed to exercise faith in that promise. The stage is then set for the believer to possess his possessions. Promises represent the future (what potentially will be) and are either stated explicitly in the future tense ("will" or "shall") or are implied as being future because of a condition that must first be met.

How do we obtain promises? At this juncture it is fair to ask what the difference is between *claiming* and *obtaining*. Obtaining simply involves one additional step of faith to that of claiming. The previous chapter shows how claiming facts involves the faith steps of taking what God has provided and then acting accordingly. But since promises speak of future potentiality rather than present reality, you cannot start with the step of taking. It is impossible to take something that does not yet exist. The first step of faith in obtaining a promise is fulfilling the required condition.

Often the condition is simply *asking*; when no condition is explicitly stated, it usually implies that God is waiting for us to ask for it. Then He bestows the promise so that we can take it and act on it.

Let's consider three examples of obtaining promises—the first involving a specific condition that must be met, the second involving the explicit condition of asking and the third involving both an explicit and implicit condition of asking.

Example 1: When Forgiveness and Cleansing Are Needed

The first example demonstrates a promise with a specific condition that must first be met. To access the provision you must first face the promise and then obtain it.

Face the promise (the future potentiality of what will be*)*

If we stumble by yielding to the world, the flesh and/ or the devil, we need forgiveness and cleansing. Thankfully there is a glorious provision for this in the great promise of First John 1:9: "If we confess our sins, he is faithful and just to forgive us our sins, and to cleanse us from all unrighteousness." If we "confess our sins" (get honest with God accurately, thoroughly and without justifying our error by making excuses), God is "faithful" every time and "just" (because we have been justified positionally) "to forgive us our sins" (releasing us from our debt) "and to cleanse us from all unrighteousness" (giving us a clean heart). Having been cleansed, we are restored back to fellowship with God (1 John 1:7). What an amazing promise of mercy and grace! Face the promise—God forgives and cleanses you when you truly confess your sins.

Obtain the promise (as your future experience)

Once you face the promise you must obtain it. But how do you obtain the potential provision? Three steps of faith comprise the obtaining.

First, *meet the condition* by truly confessing your sins. Second, *take* God at His word that He has then forgiven you and cleansed you by thanking Him for forgiveness and cleansing. Third, *act* upon it by proceeding with the confidence of having a clean heart, not because you necessarily feel it but because God promised it. By applying these faith steps, you obtain this great promise in keeping with Hebrews 11:33: "who through faith . . . obtained promises."

As I grew in the Lord, I developed a sensitive conscience that sometimes became oversensitive. I learned early the need to confess my sins. So I would confess my sins—and keep confessing them over and over again.

I did this because the "accuser of the brethren" would whisper, "That was too easy. You must confess that again." When I did, I listened to the wrong voice, stepped backward into unbelief and failed to obtain the full blessing of the promise. I needed to take the clean heart God promised and proceed in peace.

Never to confess when you have sinned is unbelief. But when you do apply the first faith step of confession, God promises to forgive and cleanse. The implication is that this forgiveness and cleansing occurs immediately upon real confession. Then you must apply the second faith step of taking God at His word. You must take the clean heart that God promised to those who confess. If, instead, you continue to confess without any new issue of stumbling, you are stepping backward into unbelief. Rather, take the clean heart by saying, "Thank you, Lord, for a clean heart." Then you may proceed with the third faith step of acting in the confidence that the cloud has been lifted and you are restored to fellowship with God.

Example 2: When Wisdom Is Needed

The second example demonstrates a promise with the explicit condition of *asking*. Again, to access the promise you must first face the promise and then obtain it.

Face the promise (the future potentiality of what will be)

James 1:5 plainly states, "If any of you lack wisdom, let him ask of God, that giveth to all men liberally, and upbraideth not; and it shall be given him." The future tense of the word "shall" reveals that this provision is a promise, not a fact. Have you ever needed wisdom? I do often and for a variety of issues. We all regularly need new fresh impartations of "wisdom that is from above." New situations arise where divine wisdom is vital to a successful outcome.

According to this promise, we can simply "ask" God for the wisdom needed. Since He gives to all generously and without reproaching those who ask, the wisdom "shall be given." What an exceedingly great and precious promise!

Obtain the promise (as your future experience)

How do you obtain this promise? This text unfolds three steps of faith.

The first step is clear: *ask*. Simply "ask of God." However, it is not a matter of perfunctory duty. James 1:6 continues by clarifying, "But let him ask in faith, nothing wavering." To ask God rightly is to recognize that God is the provider and has promised to provide the wisdom being requested. Therefore, ask in the confidence that "it shall be given" you. Wisdom will be granted. This is the sure word of God.

Second, *take* God at His word. Since God gives to all men "liberally" or generously, and "upbraideth not" or without reproach, the implication is that God bestows the wisdom without delay regarding its time demand. Assuming you are right with God, for "If I regard iniquity in my heart, the Lord will not hear me," God gives wisdom to those who ask. Take God at His word by saying, "Thank you, Lord."

Third, *act* in the confidence that the wisdom is being supplied.

It works like this: "Lord, You know I desperately need wisdom for this occasion. Lord, without You, I'll surely make a mess of things. O Lord, please grant me wisdom from above." This is the first step of *asking*. Then as you are praying, the Spirit will bear witness with your spirit, "Here it is. Your request for wisdom is granted." At that moment take the provision by genuinely saying, "Thank you, Lord, for giving me Your wisdom for this occasion." This is the second step of *taking*. Then proceed in the confidence that the Spirit of wisdom is imparting to you divine wisdom as needed for the occasion. This is third step of *acting*.

If you never ask for wisdom, you are self-dependent. This is tragic unbelief. While you may not disbelieve God regarding wisdom, you are unbelieving if you do not ask for it. Asking for wisdom reveals God-dependence.

Once the Spirit bears witness with your spirit that you have been given what you requested, then you must take the wisdom. The Spirit's witness is more of a knowledge than a feeling. We know this because "the Spirit . . . beareth witness with our spirit, that we are [whether we feel like it or not] the children of God" (Rom. 8:16). The Spirit witnesses to your spirit. This is deeper than the soulish level of feelings. But when the Spirit does communicate to you that you have been given your request, you must take it. To keep asking at that point would be to step backward into unbelief. Take God at His word, thanking Him for His gift of wisdom.

Then proceed with confidence in God's ability, not yours. If you don't, you are once again stepping backward into unbelief. But as you act upon the promise, God is always true to His word.

This promise is a great one to possess, for wisdom is so often needed in marriage, child-training, counseling, ministry and so forth.

Example 3: When Empowerment Is Needed

The third example, by referencing two different promises for the same provision, demonstrates both an explicit and implicit condition of asking. To access this necessary provision, face the promises and then obtain them.

Face the promises (the future potentiality of what **will be***)*

In Luke 11:13 Jesus Himself gives us a vital promise regarding empowerment for service, "If ye then, being evil, know how to give good gifts unto your children: how much more shall your heavenly Father give the Holy Spirit to them that ask him?" The word "shall" reveals that this is a promise. The word "ask" reveals the condition to the promise. The phrase "the Holy Spirit" reveals what is being promised.

However, the issue here is not asking for the indwelling of the Spirit. That is a fact for every believer. The issue is asking for the power of the Holy Spirit. Our English translations insert the definite article "the" for grammatical clarity, but in the original Greek it is actually absent before the name "Holy Spirit." In Greek, when the definite article is absent before a proper name, it emphasizes not the person named, but the quality of the person named. Jesus was talking about asking for the quality of the Holy Spirit, or Holy Spirit-ness. The issue is the ministry of the Spirit—His operation and, therefore, power.

Also, the words "ask" and "give" are in the present tense, indicating that this is a promise that may be repeatedly obtained. Therefore, this is not a matter of a once-for-all second blessing, but a matter of repeatedly accessing your first blessing. The promise is literally "how much more shall your heavenly Father give, and keep giving, Holy Spirit-ness to those who ask, and keep asking."

The phrase "how much more" compares the human with the divine. "If a son shall ask bread of any of you that is a father, will he give him a stone? Or if he ask a fish, will he for a fish give him a serpent? Or if he shall ask an egg, will he offer him a scorpion? If ye then, being evil, know how to give good gifts unto your children: *how much more* shall your heavenly Father give the Holy Spirit to them that ask him?" (Luke 11:11–13). The analogy is powerful. If a human father "being evil" knows how to give good gifts, specifically food, to his children who simply ask for it, "how much more" shall your heavenly Father give the bread of His Spirit to His children who ask? Also, the implication is that there is no time delay, for a human father would not delay providing food for his hungry children when he had it at hand.

Another great promise in regard to power for service is spoken by Christ in John 7:37–39:

> In the last day, that great day of the feast, Jesus stood and cried, saying, If any man thirst, let him come unto me, and drink. He that believeth on me, as the scripture hath said, out of his belly shall flow rivers of living water. But this spake he of the Spirit, which they that believe on him should receive: for the Holy Ghost was not yet given; because that Jesus was not yet glorified.

The word "shall" reveals this is a promise. The phrase "He that believeth on me" reveals the condition to the promise. The phrase "out of his belly [from his innermost being] shall flow rivers of living water" reveals what is being promised. The "rivers of living water" refer to the ministry of the Spirit as the next verse gone on to explain. This is the Spirit-filled life for service.

Facts provide the foundation of faith for holiness or "being" right. Promises provide the foundation of faith for service or "doing" right. Facts reveal God's provision for you. Promises reveal God's provision through you to others. Luke 11:13 and John 7:37–39 are great promises for empowered service.

Obtain the promises (as your future experience)

How do you obtain these promises? Once again, three steps of faith may be understood from Luke 11:13 and implied from John 7:37–39.

First, *ask* "your heavenly Father" to "give [the] Holy Spirit" to you for the scenario for which you need the quality of the Spirit. It may be the quality of the Spirit for a witnessing opportunity or the quality of the Spirit for a child-training situation. But the first step of faith is to ask for the ministry of the Spirit. Simply ask.

Second, *take*, because Jesus emphasizes "how much more shall your heavenly Father give [the] Holy Spirit to them that ask him." Since the Father gives Holy Spirit-ness to those who ask, at that point you must take. You must transact with God regarding the promise.

Third, *act* upon the provision. Proceed in the confidence that the Spirit's power will meet you in the moment of service, regardless of how you feel prior to that moment.

Obtaining these promises might begin like this: "Lord, I need Your touch to declare the gospel on this visit. O Lord, without You I can do nothing. But I am trusting You to enable me to speak and to enable those to whom I speak to hear with understanding. Lord, I simply ask for the quality of Your Spirit in every regard." This is the first step of *asking*.

Then as you are praying, the Spirit will bear witness with your spirit, "You have your request—here it is," and you can stop asking. In fact, to keep asking would be to step backward into unbelief. Just take God at His word. Jesus promised to give Holy Spirit-ness to those who ask, and the Holy Spirit has borne witness that you have been given your request. Instead of continuing to ask, you might simply say, "Thank you, Lord, for granting me the quality of Your Spirit." This is the second step of *taking*.

While many of God's children fail to ever ask for the ministry of the Spirit, others who do learn to ask often fail to take. My son often asks for a treat, usually candy. If I see that we are far enough away from the next meal, so that he and I do not get in trouble, I will hold out to him some candy. At that point, if he were to continue to ask for candy, it would be an insult. All he needs to do is take the candy, and he has never failed to do just that. Likewise, you must take God at His word and say, "Thank you!"

Then you must proceed in the confidence that God will enable you to speak and enable those to whom you speak to hear with understanding. In other words, you must declare the gospel. You must not just believe that God can enable, but that He will as you open your mouth with the message of the good news. This is the third step of *acting*. As you take this step, God meets you in the moment of the step of faith and supernaturally enables you.

The three steps combined fulfill the condition "He that believeth on me" and obtains the promise of "rivers of living water" flowing through you to others who are in need of spiritual life.

Since "all the promises of God in him are yea, and in him Amen, unto the glory of God by us" (2 Cor. 1:20), the promises of God should inspire us to possess them by faith. We should heartily let the Holy Spirit convince us of the many "exceeding great and precious promises." May it be said of us as it was said of Abraham, "And being fully persuaded that, what he had promised, he was able also to perform" (Rom. 4:21).

Dare to face the facts and claim what is, and dare to face the promises and obtain what will be. Dare to possess your possessions! For as Joshua 13:1 declares, "there remaineth yet very much land to be possessed."

So far we have looked at promises that state or imply an immediate answer. It is fair to ask, how does faith operate when an immediate answer is not stated or implied? We will address that issue in Chapter Six. But first, let's look at how facing facts and obtaining promises in faith makes a difference in our prayer life.

Chapter Five

The Prayer of Faith:
Biblical Foundation

And the prayer of faith shall save the sick. The effectual fervent prayer of a righteous man availeth much.

James 5:15–16

In 1966 our family moved from Durango, Colorado to Chicago, Illinois. Being only four years old at the time, I had no idea how significant this move was, but for my oldest brother, Wayne, it was a radical cultural shift. To go from the cowboy boots, horses, ranches and ski slopes of Colorado to the city limits of Chicago's south side in the 1960s was indeed a change.

The youth of the church that my father came to pastor were not in the best of shape spiritually. As a young teen, Wayne went to a public school and did well in basketball. By age fifteen, although he did not get involved in the wickedness around him, nevertheless my parents began to notice the draw of the world on his young heart. So my father called my grandmother (his mother) because she knew how to pray. My grandmother immediately began to seek God's face about the matter.

At that time Dad was planning to go on one of his trips to the Bible Lands. After seeking God's face, my grandmother called my father and, with joy, announced that she had met with God, that my brother was going to go with Dad on his trip to Israel, and that God was going to use this trip to get a hold of his heart and change his life.

Respectfully my father said that it was not possible for Wayne to go with him to Israel because there were no more seats available on the flight. Even if there were seats available, he really did not have the money to buy the ticket, and there would not be enough time to get the passport for Wayne anyway. However, my grandmother responded saying that she had met with God, that Wayne would go on that trip with my father and that through it all God was going to change his life! Then she went back to rejoicing and praising the Lord.

My father knew from experience that when his mother spoke with that kind of confidence, whatever she had received from the Lord would occur. Within a few days a man scheduled to go on that trip got quite ill. He decided to give his ticket to my brother. They worked out the transfer, got Wayne's passport, and Wayne went on that trip.

At the Garden Tomb, during a message preached while the tour group listened with the empty tomb in view, the Lord began to speak to my brother's heart. While there, my aunt, who was also on this trip, went into the tomb behind Wayne. She said that he gazed at the empty slab, and when he finally turned around there were tears streaming down his face. The reality that Jesus is alive and that He is worth living for struck a deep chord within his heart.

Immediately after returning home, Wayne surrendered to the call to preach. Then God set his heart on fire. Although shy by personality, he became a bold witness for Christ in the public school. The fire began to spread in the church youth group. Soon Bible studies and prayer meetings were organized within the public schools by the church teens who attended the various schools on Chicago's south side.

As a boy, I remember hearing the teens talk about loving Jesus, and using expressions like "What a blessing this or that was!" and "Praise the Lord that so-and-so got saved!" God had ignited a revival in the youth group, one that began within my brother's heart—and all because of a prayer that made a difference!

Since the effectual, fervent prayer of a righteous man makes a difference, we must learn to pray the prayer of faith. What is involved in the prayer of faith? In this chapter we will discuss its biblical foundation, and in the next chapter we will address its practical phases. For now, what constitutes the biblical foundation of the prayer of faith? Three connected truths within the Scripture provide the answer.

Divine Purposes

First, God has divine purposes. This is a matter of God's *will*. First John 5:14 begins by saying, "And this is the confidence that we have in him, that, if we ask any thing *according to his will*, he heareth us." Clearly, God has a will—a sovereign will.

However, contrary to the thinking of some, God's will is not automatic or inevitable. The Lord's Prayer proves that this is the case because Jesus said, "Thy will be done on earth as it is in heaven." Why would Jesus lead us to pray this if God's will is automatic or inevitable? The fact is that God's will is often *not* being done on earth as it is in heaven. Just take a look around!

S.D. Gordon, in his *Quiet Talks on Prayer*, emphasizes that there are only two wills: God's will and Satan's will.[1] Some may wonder, "What about man's will?" The will of man either lines up with God's will or Satan's will. This is a sobering thought.

For example, in the matter of salvation, God "will have all men to be saved, and to come unto the knowledge of the truth" (1 Tim. 2:4). Plainly, salvation is God's will for "all men," but do all men get saved? The answer is obvious. Is it possible to miss out on God's will for salvation? Again the answer ought to be obvious.

Peter affirms that "The Lord is . . . not willing that any should perish, but that all should come to repentance" (2 Pet. 3:9). Is it God's will that "all should come to repentance"? This is what the plain words claim. But do all come to repentance? Sadly, many do not. Is it possible to miss out on God's will for salvation? Again the answer is clear.

God has a sovereign will, but man can miss out on that will. What is true in salvation is also true in sanctification and service. For example, Psalm 78:41 states that Israel's unbelief in the wilderness "limited the Holy One of Israel." The word "limited" implies Israel missed out on God's will. Obviously God allowed it, and His sovereignty is not diminished. But that generation missed His will for them. Referring to Jesus in His "own country," Matthew 13:58 declares, "And he did not many mighty works there because of their unbelief." The implication is clear. His will was to do much more, but unbelief caused those involved to miss out on His will.

The concept that God's will is sovereign but not automatic may shake some theological grids. Yet if words have meaning and language has integrity, then it is clear from these passages that it is possible to miss out on the will of God for one's life. So how can we be sure that God's will is "done on earth as it is in heaven"?

Scriptural Promises

The second connected truth is that God's divine purposes are revealed through scriptural promises. This is a matter of God's *word*. God's Word reveals His will. His promises reveal His purposes.

But how does God give you a particular scriptural promise? In other words, how do you know if you may stand on a specific promise for a specific occasion? Do you randomly choose a promise, or is there more to it? The answer to these questions lies in how the Spirit of truth works in your life through the Word of truth. Jesus said the Spirit "will guide you into all truth" (John 16:13). Sometimes there are other issues involved in knowing the will of God, but the basic key is the Word and the Spirit.

The Word

The fuel of faith is the Word of God. This cannot be overemphasized. As mentioned in Chapter Two, Romans 10:17 says, "So then faith cometh by hearing, and hearing by the word of God." We noted that the term "word" is *rhema* emphasizing a specific word of God. But how do you know if you may legitimately "stand" on a specific word for a specific occasion?

The Spirit

Since the Spirit "will guide you into all truth," we must trust the Spirit to guide us to the specific truth appropriate to a specific situation. In other words, we must be "looking unto Jesus, the author and finisher of our faith" (Heb. 12:2). Since Jesus is the living Word, there is a mystery of oneness between the Incarnate Word, Christ, and the written Word, the Scriptures. As we look unto Jesus by seeking Him in the sacred text, the Spirit of Jesus "authors" faith in our hearts by convincing us not only of the truth, but of the relevancy of that truth for the specific need we have. This is the "evidence" needed to depend on the reality of the words of God (Heb. 11:1).

In chapter two we noted that the word "evidence" in Hebrews 11:1 is the noun form of the verb "reprove" in John 16:8, which speaks of the Spirit proving or convincing the world of sin, righteousness and judgment. The Holy Spirit is the "Convincer." When He illumines a *rhema* to your heart and convinces you that you may stand on that specific word for a given situation, you have the evidence needed to exercise faith. This is the combination of the Word and the Spirit revealing to you God's will for a given burden. It is the Spirit bearing witness with your spirit. This "witness" is more of a knowledge than a feeling. For example, Romans 8:16 says, "The Spirit beareth witness with our spirit, that we are [not that we "feel like"] the children of God." This is not a soul-level feeling, but a spirit-level knowledge; it is not looking within yourself, but unto Jesus as the "author" of your faith.

Focusing on the object of faith is the key; focusing on the subject of faith is a killer. In other words, focusing on your need of "conviction" is a hindrance, but focusing on the object of faith as the answer to your need is a help. This cannot be over-emphasized. Some get derailed because they look inward rather than upward. They know they need Spirit-conviction, but they unwittingly look inward for the sense of conviction, instead of looking unto Jesus (the Word and the Spirit) for the evidence needed to proceed in the confidence of God's will. As you focus on the Word, the Spirit will convince according to the will of God.

Frankly, the process is much simpler than some make it out to be. Just focus on the Faithful One, and the needed guidance will be given. If you get introspective, however, you open the door for Satanic counterfeit or self-deception, such as confusing your own strong desire for something as the Holy Spirit's conviction. If this occurs, don't let yourself get disillusioned and drop out of the race of faith (Heb. 12:1–2). Simply humble yourself and say, "Lord, I got it wrong. Please teach me, and don't let me deceive myself or get deceived. I trust Your ability to speak, not my ability to listen." God will then heal your broken wings of faith and lead you along.

My grandmother, Oma Van Gelderen, was by God's grace a mighty prayer warrior, yet with simple child-like faith. As a result, people would call her and ask her to pray. Once a missionary asked her to pray that God would heal a certain leper. She prayed—and God healed the leper.

When my grandmother talked to the Lord, she spoke to Him as if He was right there—because He was. Often when she prayed, the tears rolled down her cheeks as she quickly slipped "within the veil" to the manifest presence of God. She had *real* fellowship with God.

For years my grandmother lived with my aunt. I once asked my aunt, "What did Grandma do when people asked her to pray about something? I know she prayed. But how did she go about it?"

My aunt said that she took her well-worn Bible, sat down in a certain spot on the sofa and began to talk to the Lord, saying something along these lines: "Lord, I know that nothing is impossible with You. You can meet this need. But I need to know Your will on the matter. Show me what You want to do and, therefore, what I can have confidence to expect."

She would then look into her Bible. Sometimes she would look to a promise that the Lord had spoken to her before regarding a similar burden to see if the Lord would "give life" to that promise again. Sometimes God did. Other times God led her to a "new" promise.

The point is that she knew she had to discover the will of God through the Word and the Spirit so that she could have confidence in prayer. She understood the truth of First John 5:14–15: "And this is the confidence that we have in him, that, if we ask any thing according to his will, he heareth us: And if we know that he hear us, whatsoever we ask, we know that we have the petitions that we desired of him."

God has divine purposes, and scriptural promises reveal His divine purposes. It might seem that once you have a scriptural promise revealing God's purpose, the matter is settled. But there is one more connected truth.

Believing Prayer

Third, God's promises must be obtained by faith. This is a matter of God's *way*. God is sovereign over all; He is in control. But in His sovereign wisdom, God chose to make man responsible to come into union with His will, by means of faith, before He performs certain things. God's sovereign way is to reveal His will through the Word and the Spirit, and make man responsible to access His will through faith. God then responds to those who respond to Him.

God's promises are not automatic. They are potentialities that must be obtained. As it says in the "Hall of Faith" chapter, God was pleased by those "who through faith . . . obtained promises" (Heb. 11:33).Though some promises will be received only after we are glorified (see 11:36–40), many promises are to be obtained now. This is how God in His sovereignty chose to work. What a privilege, and yet, what a responsibility!

James 4:2 simply states, "ye have not, because ye ask not," and the next verse warns that God will not answer your prayer if "ye ask amiss." But if you are seeking God's *divine purposes* as revealed through *His scriptural promises*, you are asking according to the will of God, so you need not worry that you are asking "amiss." If you are not receiving something that God has promised, it is not because you are asking amiss—it is because *you are not asking at all!* You can miss out on God's will through the unbelief of not asking.

There are blessings you could be enjoying right now, James implies, but you are not, simply because you have not asked. A veteran pastor once told me, "One of the greatest regrets I believe I will have when I get to heaven is to find out all that was God's will for me that I missed out on because I did not ask." This is a sobering possibility.

The pattern of faith is spelled out Second Peter 1:3–4:

> According as his divine power hath given unto us all things that pertain unto life and godliness, through the knowledge of him that hath called us to glory and virtue [God's *will*]: whereby are given unto us exceeding great and precious promises [God's *word*]: that by these ye might be partakers of the divine nature, having escaped the corruption that is in the world through lust [God's *way*].

First John 5:14–15 also makes the pattern clear: "*if we ask* anything according to his will . . . we have the petitions that we desired of him." Some people never take the time to let the Holy Spirit reveal to them God's promises from His storehouse of blessing. Others see the promises, yet fail to exercise faith. They fail to take even the first step of faith regarding a promise: to ask. Consequently, they often get disillusioned because the promises do not come to pass. But they do not realize their own responsibility in the matter.

Our will apart from God's will is a hindrance to prayer (James 4:3). God's will apart from our will is a limitation to action (James 4:2; Ps. 78:11). But our will united to God's will is the key to God's action in answer to our prayer (1 John 5:14–15).

A promise reveals the purpose of the one giving the promise. But a promise also demands faith from the one receiving the promise. When a parent promises a child something special on a certain day, the parent's promise reveals the parent's will or purpose. But it demands faith on the part of the child.

For example, my young son loves to go to the toy store. Occasionally I will promise my son, "Hey, John, tomorrow Daddy is going to take you to the toy store." This promise reveals my purpose, but it demands faith on his part. Do you think he remembers my promise? When he wakes up the next morning, he will ask something like, "When are we going to the toy store? Daddy, you said we would go to the toy store. Are we going to go now, Daddy?" This is his expression of dependence to "obtain" the promise.

Similarly our loving, heavenly Father gives us promises that reveal His will. But He waits for us to say, "Daddy, You said . . . ." This pleases Him as we show our dependence on His will and power.

Divine purposes are like checks in God's checkbook. Scriptural promises are like signed checks through the Word and the Spirit. Believing prayer is like cashing the checks. Amazingly, God has chosen to accomplish many of His purposes through the believing partnership of His people. In Ezekiel 36 God promises, "I will . . . " regarding a number of blessings He intends for His people, but then He makes clear, "I will yet for this be enquired of . . . to do it for them" (Ezek. 36:37).

In this chapter we have discussed the biblical foundation for the prayer of faith. What we have seen coincides with the emphasis noted in Chapter Three regarding possessing *promises*. But some promises do not state or imply that they will occur immediately. Practically, how does faith operate when this is the case? The next chapter seeks to answer this question.

Chapter Six

The Prayer of Faith:
Practical Phases

*Is any among you afflicted? let him pray. Is any merry? let
him sing psalms. Is any sick among you? let him call for the
elders of the church; and let them pray over him, anointing
him with oil in the name of the Lord: and the prayer of faith
shall save the sick, and the Lord shall raise him up; and if he
have committed sins, they shall be forgiven him. Confess your
faults one to another, and pray one for another, that ye may
be healed. The effectual fervent prayer of a righteous man
availeth much. Elias was a man subject to like passions as
we are, and he prayed earnestly that it might not rain: and
it rained not on the earth by the space of three years and six
months. And he prayed again, and the heaven gave rain, and
the earth brought forth her fruit.*

James 5:13–18

Since the effectual fervent prayer of a righteous man
makes a difference, we must learn to pray the prayer of
faith. What is involved in the prayer of faith? The previous

chapter discussed its biblical foundation, and this chapter addresses its practical phases.

The concept of the prayer of faith does not apply to every kind of praying. Often there is an immediate need, a simple prayer to our loving Father in heaven, and a quick answer. This is a wonderful privilege for God's children and a major part of our daily walk with God. In addition, you may already have light from the Lord about His will in certain areas and may repeatedly trust the Lord for those matters.

However, occasionally the type of need and the dynamics that accompany that need demand "the effectual fervent prayer of a righteous man" that "availeth much." This is what is known as the prayer of faith, and it involves three phases.

1. Praying *to* the Promise

The first phase is a matter of allowing the Spirit to guide you to the truth that is the foundation of faith for a given special need. Praying *to* the promise is praying until the Holy Spirit convinces you that you may stand on a given promise for a given situation. It is praying until you "see" the evidence through Spirit-conviction of a specific truth.

Some people's prayers are little more than wishful thinking, but real faith arises when you are convinced of God's will. This is not a matter of "name it/claim it." This is a matter of letting *God* name it so that you may claim it. To attempt to force your will on God is presumption. But to not take the time to get the mind of the Lord is unbelief. It is not a matter of saying, "God, here is what I want You to do." It is a matter of saying, "God, here is my need. What do You want to do? What may I expect You to do? I know you can meet the need, but I need to know if You will."

Praying *to* the promise is looking unto Jesus that He might author faith in your heart through Holy Spirit-conviction of His promise for a specific situation. This may be described as "coming to faith" regarding a given matter. For example, many are convinced generally of God's promise that He is "not willing that any should perish, but that all should come to repentance" (2 Pet. 3:9). But there is a difference between being convinced of that promise *generally* (because of the Word of God) and being convinced of that promise *specifically* for a given person (because of the Spirit of God). This distinction must be grasped in order to move forward in faith regarding the lost.

It is in this first phase that God may adjust our praying "for we know not what we should pray for as we ought," and the Spirit "with groanings which cannot be uttered" guides us into "the mind of the Spirit" which, of course, is "according to the will of God" (Rom. 8:26–27). Sometimes it is a matter of "fine-tuning." Other times it is a matter of redirecting. When Paul prayed for his "thorn in the flesh" to be removed, God redirected him by letting him know His purpose in not relieving Paul of that difficulty. But when you have the mind of the Lord, then you can pray with confidence that God will answer because you are praying according to the will of God.

Once when I was preaching on this subject in a local church, a lady told me that she had prayed for two sick loved ones to be healed. But both times she prayed for this, the loved ones died. This lady then said that she got disillusioned and virtually stopped praying. However, she said with tears in her eyes that now she realized that she had no basis for her prayers. She had never sought the mind of the

Lord. In other words, she had no conviction to be able to pray the prayer of faith.

James A. Stewart, an evangelist from Scotland, saw the Lord bless in great revival and harvest blessing in Eastern Europe before and after World War II. He would often pray over a map of the region. As God burdened him with special mission projects, he would pray for the needed finances. His wife writes:

> But there were the special seasons when James felt the Lord would have us take on a large "project" on the mission field which required a sum of money far exceeding his own faith at the time. He had to pray for faith. He had to wrestle before the Lord and pray himself "into faith." At times he began praying alone and then would come to me with "come help me pray. I can claim from the Lord thus and so, but I have not yet faith to claim the full amount needed." At such times I would witness those wrestlings before the Lord which were the secret of his life of faith. He would cry, "YOU ARE GOD! YOU CAN DO ANYTHING! You can do this, You want to do this for your glory. Now give me the faith to claim it from your hand." And He did. James could often tell when the money would arrive and how much would be in the letter or on the check; such confidence had been given him by His Father.[1]

Stewart understood that the greatest wrestling in prayer was what we are terming here "praying *to* the promise." He knew that this first phase really was the greatest "wrestling" because once he had the mind of the Lord, he knew from experience that it was a done deal. If he would but pray on that basis, God would come through with the answer.

Some people never wrestle in prayer; they never take the time or effort involved in praying *to* the promise. They are just playing, not praying. Others may pray fervently, but often interpret their own strong desire as the Holy Spirit's leading, or confuse their own logical assumptions for conviction, or add details to the promise that the Lord did not give. I cannot caution you enough to listen for God's voice as you wrestle in prayer.

Praying *to* the promise is praying until the Holy Spirit "authors" faith in your heart by convincing you of His promise for a given situation. In the spiritual realm it is as if the Spirit holds out to you that for which you are seeking. This then opens the door for the second phase.

2. The Prayer of the Faith Based *on* the Promise

In James 5:15 the literal wording includes a definite article not only before the word "prayer," but also before the word "faith." The wording is literally "the prayer of the faith." This is a specific prayer offered with a specific faith. The prayer of faith is a transaction with God whereby in the spiritual realm you take that which the Holy Spirit is holding out to you. It is simply a matter of praying "the prayer of the faith" based *on* the promise that the Spirit has given you through the Word. The prayer of faith is the bold taking of what God is giving because you are convinced that He is giving it.

James O. Fraser, pioneer missionary to western China, prayed for four years that God would save hundreds of Lisu families. During this time the Lord was patiently teaching His servant. This is what Fraser learned:

Faith is like muscle which grows stronger and stronger with use, rather than rubber, which weakens when it is stretched. . . . Overstrained faith is not pure faith; there is a mixture of the carnal element in it. There is no strain in the "rest of faith." It asks for definite blessings as God may lead. It does not hold back through carnal timidity, nor press ahead too far through carnal eagerness. . . . Unanswered prayers have taught me to seek the Lord's will instead of my own. . . . Many "good desires" proceed from our uncrucified selves. . . . When we once have the deep, calm assurance of his will in the matter, we put in our claim, just as a child before his father. A simple request and nothing more. No cringing, no beseeching, no tears, no wrestling. No second asking either.[2]

In Fraser's own words, he testifies of praying the prayer of faith:

In my case I prayed continually for the Tengyueh Lisu for over four years, asking many times that several hundreds of families might be turned to God. This was only general prayer, however. God was dealing with me in the meantime. You know how a child is sometimes rebuked by his parents for asking something in a wrong way—perhaps in the case of a child, for asking rudely. The parent will say, "Ask me properly." That is just what God seemed to be saying to me then: "Ask me properly. You have been asking me to do this for the last four years without ever really believing that I would do it—now ask in faith."

I felt the burden clearly. I went to my room alone one afternoon and knelt in prayer. I knew that the time had come for the prayer of faith. And then, fully knowing what I was doing and what it might cost me, I definitely committed myself to this petition in faith. I cast my burden upon the Lord and rose from my knees with the deep, restful conviction that I had already received the answer. The transaction was done. And since then (nearly a year ago now) I have never had anything but peace and joy (when in touch with God) in holding to the ground already claimed and taken. I have never repeated the request and never will: there is no need. The asking, the taking and the receiving occupy but a few moments (Mark 11:24). It is a solemn thing to enter into a faith covenant with God. It is binding on both parties. You lift up your hand to God, you definitely ask for and receive his proffered gift—then do not go back on your faith, even if you live to be 100.[3]

After praying for another year from the promise through to victory, God poured out His Spirit, and hundreds of Lisu families came to Christ. But what does it mean to pray from the promise through to victory? This leads us to a third phase.

3. Praying *from* the Promise *through* to Fulfillment

While some fail to pray *to* the promise, and some fail to pray *on* the promise, others fail to pray *from* the promise *through* to fulfillment. What does this mean?

First and foremost it means praising the Lord for what He has given—rejoicing that the promise has been bestowed and received, and thanking God for His provision. All this is a matter of standing for the ground the Lord has given. It is praying because you have received your request in the spiritual realm, and since you are rejoicing in what God has given in the heavenly realm, you pray, "Thy will [now] be done on earth as it is [has been done] in heaven."

Second, praying from the promise means warring from the throne against any satanic attempt to hinder your answer from moving from the spiritual/heavenly realm to the physical/earthly realm. This is spiritual warfare. When Daniel was praying for understanding, an angel revealed to him this concept:

> Then said he unto me, Fear not, Daniel: for from the first day that thou didst set thine heart to understand, and to chasten thyself before thy God, thy words were heard, and I am come for thy words. But the prince of the kingdom of Persia withstood me one and twenty days: but, lo, Michael, one of the chief princes, came to help me; and I remained there with the kings of Persia. Now I am come to make thee understand what shall befall thy people in the latter days: for yet the vision is for many days.

While there is a standing *for* the ground God has given, there is also a standing *against* Satan's attempt to hinder God's answer from coming through. This involves claiming Christ's victory over the Enemy.

Third, praying from the promise means praying through the details of the situation as the Spirit leads, that God may receive greater glory in the fulfillment of the prayer.

To summarize, the three phases of the prayer of faith are:

- *Ask*: Keep praying until the Spirit purifies your prayer and convinces you that the request is being granted. Sometimes there may be a length of time involved.
- *Take*: When the Spirit bears witness, "You can take what you have been asking for," then you can pray "the prayer of [the] faith," *taking* God at His word. This is a definite transaction. In the spiritual realm you have the answer, even if it is not yet manifested in the physical realm.

- *Act*: Therefore, you may *act* by praying *from* the promise *through* to fulfillment. If you find yourself striving in this third phase, you may not be as convinced as you thought you were in the first phase.

Not all our prayers, and not even all prayers of faith, involve such a long-term process. But Scripture includes several extended prayers of faith, including those of David (1 Chron. 17:16–27, in response to the promise of 17:3–15) and Daniel (Dan. 9:2–3, in response to the promise of Jer. 29:10–14).

One of the most remarkable examples is found in the life of Elijah: "And Elijah the Tishbite . . . said unto Ahab, As the LORD God of Israel liveth, before whom I stand, there shall not be dew nor rain these years, but according to my word" (1 Kings 17:1). How could Elijah have such boldness? This would be like storming into the Oval Office and announcing that it will not rain in America until you say so.

How could Elijah be so bold? First Kings does not answer that question, but the New Testament does: "Elias [Elijah] was a man subject to like passions as we are, and he prayed earnestly that it might not rain: and it rained not on the earth by the space of three years and six months" (James 5:17). Elijah was no super-saint; he was just like the rest of us. But he could boldly confront Ahab with the announcement of no rain, because he had "prayed earnestly" about the matter.

Yet some people pray earnestly, even to the point of tears, for things they never receive. What was the difference with Elijah? More specifically, what was the foundation of faith for his prayer? First Kings does not reveal this; nor does

James 5. But Deuteronomy contains a clear promise concerning the issue of rain:

> And it shall come to pass, if ye shall hearken diligently unto my commandments which I command you this day, to love the LORD your God, and to serve him with all your heart and with all your soul, that I will give you the rain of your land in his due season, the first rain and the latter rain, that thou mayest gather in thy corn, and thy wine, and thine oil. And I will send grass in thy fields for thy cattle, that thou mayest eat and be full. Take heed to yourselves, that your heart be not deceived, and ye turn aside, and serve other gods, and worship them; and then the LORD's wrath be kindled against you, and he shut up the heaven, that there be no rain, and that the land yield not her fruit; and lest ye perish quickly from off the good land which the LORD giveth you. (11:13–17)

Positively, God promised that if His people loved Him and served Him wholeheartedly, He would give them rain for an abundant harvest and meet their needs. Negatively, God promised that if His people turned away from Him into idolatry, He would "shut up the heaven, that there be no rain"; their crops would fail and their needs would not be met.

At the time of Elijah, Israel had been in idolatry for some time. Jeroboam had led the northern kingdom to embrace idolatry by setting up the golden calves at Dan and Bethel when the kingdoms divided. But years later, Ahab, through his marriage with Jezebel, led Israel to worship the pagan god Baal. So Israel was in full-blown apostasy and idolatry at this time.

God said that if His people worshiped false gods, He would shut the heavens from giving rain. But promises, even negative promises, are not automatic. They must be obtained. Why did Elijah pray earnestly that it might not rain? Because it was still raining! You can almost hear Elijah's prayer: "Lord God, You said that if Your people worshiped idols, You would stop the rain to get their attention. But Lord, they keep having season after season of rain and harvest! They are going to think that You do not mean what You say. Lord, will You stop the rain to be true to Your word and to awaken Your people to turn back to You?" The implication of Elijah's bold announcement to Ahab is that God let Elijah know that he had received the answer to his fervent prayer.

Then in the third year of the famine, "the word of the LORD came to Elijah . . . I will send rain" (1 Kings 18:1). This led to Elijah's challenging the prophets of Baal at Mount Carmel. In his prayer Elijah said, "Hear me, O LORD, hear me, that this people may know that thou art the LORD God, and that thou hast turned their heart back again" (1 Kings 18:37). The negative promise of no rain that Elijah had obtained had done its work—the people were awakened back to their need of Jehovah God. The next verse then says, "Then the fire of the LORD fell," and as a result, the people cried out, "The LORD, he is the God; the LORD, he is the God" (1 Kings 18:38–39).

Now the positive promise of Deuteronomy 11 could be obtained, as well as the fresh word from the Lord, "I will send rain," which indicated that God's timing was ripe. Therefore, after announcing to Ahab that there was "a sound of abundance of rain," you might think that Elijah would go get his umbrella and wait. But that is not what he does. Instead, he prayed for rain. Why? Because he understood that promises must be obtained. So Elijah prayed with "his face between his knees" (1 Kings 18:42) and then sent his servant to look toward the sea. Clearly, Elijah expected to see rain clouds gathering. This he did seven more times. Why did Elijah keep praying? He kept praying, not because he believed God *could* send rain. That would have been in the first phase of praying. He was in the third phase. Elijah kept praying because he believed God *would* send rain. He already had the answer in heaven. It was now simply a matter of God's will being done on earth. Once Elijah became aware of "a little cloud . . . like a man's hand," he knew the answer had been manifested. He had prayed from the promise through to fulfillment.

For many years my wife, Mary Lynn, and I could not have children. Then after thirteen years, we were with Pastor Charlie Kittrell of Indianapolis, Indiana for a week of revival meetings. Charlie Kittrell was a prayer warrior. When he prayed, he would say, "Lord, if You'll do it, I'll tell it to Your honor and glory." Consequently, when you were around him, he often related glorious answers to prayer. He would get on a theme and then tell a series of illustrations of how God had answered prayer. One day during our week with him, he told stories of couples who could not have children, but who had asked him to anoint them with oil and pray for a child. He related couple after couple where this was done, and then God gave them a child or children. Several of these couples were people we knew.

Later on, my wife said to me, "Do you think that I should ask Pastor Kittrell to anoint me with oil and pray for a child?" I replied, "You can if you want to." So she did. Unknown to us until later, Charlie Kittrell had been praying that Mary Lynn would do this. Therefore, when she did, he had conviction from the Lord that God intended to give us a child.

Pastor Kittrell came to our recreational vehicle with a small bottle of oil. He explained that there was nothing magical in the oil, but that we were simply depending on God's Word according to James 5. Then he asked my wife, "Now, do you want a son or a daughter?" Mary Lynn immediately replied, "A son." He replied, "Good, that's what I was hoping you would say!" He probably had prayed about that too.

Then he put a little oil on the tip of his finger, placed it on Mary Lynn's head and very simply prayed that God would give us a son. The prayer was not fancy, and there was nothing dramatic about the whole scene. He simply prayed *the prayer of faith*.

Two years passed. My wife and I thought, "Charlie Kittrell gets it right most of the time, but maybe he got it wrong on this one." I suppose you could call this unbelief. But about this time Pastor Kittrell preached in my home church in Ann Arbor, Michigan for a New Year's Eve service. We were not at this service, being away in our travels. But he boldly announced to my home church that God was giving us a son. At that point, this was after fifteen years of marriage with no children.

Yet another year passed, making it sixteen years with no children. Then a friend of mine, who was in Indianapolis on business, attended Charlie Kittrell's church on a Sunday morning. Evidently Pastor Kittrell said something that made my friend think that Mary Lynn was pregnant. So my friend called his wife on the phone and asked her, "Is Mary Lynn expecting?" His wife replied, "No, she couldn't be. We are in touch regularly, and I'm sure she would have told me if she were." He said, "Well, it sure sounded like it from what Charlie Kittrell said."

Amazingly, at that moment my wife, Mary Lynn, was in fact expecting—but we did not even know it. When the burden lifted from Charlie Kittrell's heart, he knew that the answer had moved from heaven to earth. This is one way that "The secret of the Lord is with them that fear him" (Ps. 25:14).

Later that week we discovered that Mary Lynn was expecting a baby. On returning from a doctor's visit that confirmed our discovery, the first person I called was Charlie Kittrell. Of course, he already knew, but I did not know that. When I informed him of God's answer to prayer, he genuinely rejoiced with us. I was expressing my shock and surprise which is really unbelief. He simply said, "John, I never stop believing!" Why? Because he had prayed *to* the promise, prayed the prayer of the faith based *on* the promise, and had prayed *from* the promise *through* to victory. It was prayer that made a difference!

Since the effectual fervent prayer of a righteous man makes a difference, we must learn to pray the prayer of faith.

Chapter Seven

The Increase of Faith

And the apostles said unto the Lord, Increase our faith.
Luke 17:5

When people with a heart for God study the lives of those who have experienced faith in God—ordinary people who learned to trust in an extraordinary God—they can't help but join the apostles in the heartcry, "Increase our faith." The Greek word for "increase" can also mean "to add to, to give in addition."[1] Jesus uses the same word in the phrase "and all these things shall be *added unto* you" (Matt. 6:33). The word is used in recounting the results of the Day of Pentecost "and the same day there were *added unto* them about three thousand souls" (Acts 2:41). But what does it mean to increase your faith?

When Paul writes to the Corinthians, he uses the terminology "when your faith is increased" (2 Cor. 10:15). The word "increased," a synonym to the word we just noted, means "to grow, to increase."[2] This word occurs in the phrases "Consider the lilies . . . how they *grow*" (Matt. 6:28), "the child *grew*" (Luke 1:80), "the word of God *increased*" (Acts 6:7), "He must *increase*" (John 3:30), and "*grow* in grace" (2 Pet. 3:18). But what does it mean to increase your faith?

Paul rejoices with gratitude as he writes to the Thessalonians "because your faith groweth exceedingly" (2 Thess. 1:3). The verb noted above that Paul used with the Corinthians is here used in compound with a preposition meaning "to greatly increase."[3] This is the only time this compound is used in the New Testament, and it is used to describe faith increasing greatly. But yet again, what does it mean to increase your faith?

Since the Scripture indicates the possibility of a growing faith or a faith that increases, we must join in the heartcry, "Lord, increase our faith." But what is the nature of the increase, especially as it relates to faith? The answer depends on the aspect of the increase to which one is referring.

The word "great" is used in conjunction with the word "faith" three times in the New Testament, incorporating two Greek words conveying the idea of "great." The word "little" is used in compound with the word "faith" five times in the New Testament. By itself and when the object being described is singular, the word "little" means "little, small, short" with the possibilities "of quantity," "of degree," or "of duration."[4] Interestingly, all of the "great faith" and "little faith" references are found in Matthew with the exception of one parallel account of "great faith" found in Luke. A careful study of these and other related passages reveals that there are three ways that faith may be increased.

Quantity of Occurrences

The most obvious way faith may be increased is an increase in the quantity of occurrences for which faith is exercised. For example, when addressing daily and repetitive needs such as food and clothing, Jesus challenges His disciples not to worry but to trust in their loving and caring heavenly Father who watches over even the birds and the lilies (Matt. 6:25–29). Then Jesus kindly chides His disciples saying, "Wherefore, if God so clothes the grass of the field . . . shall he not much more clothe you, O ye of *little faith*?" (Matt. 6:30). He again confronts the unbelief of worrying and emphasizes, "But seek ye first the kingdom of God, and his righteousness; and all these things shall be added unto you" (Matt. 6:31–33). Finally, Jesus urges His disciples not to worry even about tomorrow, concluding with the words, "Sufficient unto the day is the evil [trouble] thereof" (Matt. 6:34).

You can trust God and therefore, you can trust Him daily. The verb tense of the command "seek" in Matthew 6:33 conveys the emphasis of seeking God continually. In fact, the focus is to be seeking first God's kingdom and righteousness, knowing that He will repeatedly supply your daily needs. The description of "little faith" in this context as well as the parallel passage in Luke 12:22–31 meant that the disciples needed to learn to trust in God repeatedly. They needed their faith to increase in the sense of the quantity of occurrences for which faith is exercised.

Matthew 16 provides another example of "little faith" in this same sense. Jesus had miraculously fed the five thousand and then later the four thousand. Soon after we read:

And when his disciples were come to the other side, they had forgotten to take bread. Then Jesus said unto them, Take heed and beware of the leaven of the Pharisees and of the Sadducees. And they reasoned among themselves, saying, It is because we have taken no bread. Which when Jesus perceived, he said unto them, O ye of *little faith*, why reason ye among yourselves, because ye have brought no bread? Do ye not yet understand, neither remember the five loaves of the five thousand, and how many baskets ye took up? Neither the seven loaves of the four thousand, and how many baskets ye took up? How is it that ye do not understand that I spake it not to you concerning bread, that ye should beware of the leaven of the Pharisees and of the Sadducees? Then understood they how that he bade them not beware of the leaven of bread, but of the doctrine of the Pharisees and of the Sadducees. (16:5–12)

When Jesus used the word "remember," He singled out the issue at hand. The previous miracles regarding feeding both the five thousand and four thousand should have bolstered the disciples' faith regarding any needed bread. If you have the presence of Jesus, you have His all-sufficiency. In the context, therefore, they should have known that He was not talking about physical bread but the teaching of the Pharisees. But the point is made secondarily that remembering the past provision of God should cultivate faith for the present provision of God.

The "little faith" of the disciples was little in the sense of quantity of occurrences or readiness to exercise faith again on a given issue that had already been proven. Seeing God work before, especially in a given way, should increase your faith to see Him work again in that same way. It should begin a readiness to trust Him for that issue.

Just as exercising a particular muscle strengthens it, so the spiritual exercise of faith for a particular need should strengthen our faith to believe again for that same need. As you learn to trust God for certain things, your confidence in God should grow, because God has proven Himself faithful in those areas.

As an evangelist, I preach on average nearly once a day. Over the years the promise of the Spirit's empowerment in Luke 11:13 has blessed my heart repeatedly, because I need the ministry of the Spirit every time I preach. God has provided for me in the area of preaching multitudes of times over the years, cultivating a confidence in my heart that if I trust Him for the Spirit's ministry in preaching, He will faithfully provide for me. I have seen Him answer over and over again. But there are many other areas where I need to learn to trust—and trust Him repeatedly.

As walking consists of reiterated steps, one way of increasing faith is simply in reiterated steps of faith. Faith increases quantitatively only in the sense of the quantity of occurrences for which faith is exercised. Since faith is faith, the issue of quantity is not the "size" of one's faith, but the quantity of the occurrences for which faith is exercised.

Degree of Difficulty

Another way faith may be increased is an increase in the degree of difficulty for which faith is exercised. You cannot believe harder, but there are some things that are harder to believe. New territory as yet uncharted, and therefore never before experienced, may seem a more difficult ground on which to step out in faith. But nothing is too hard for God. The hard part at times is for man to believe. He must join

Jeremiah in the exclamation, "Ah Lord GOD! behold, thou hast made the heaven and the earth by thy great power and stretched out arm, and there is nothing too hard for thee" (Jer. 32:17). Jeremiah came to this at a moment in which God was calling him to trust Him for something incredibly difficult to believe (32:6–44).

The New Testament provides both a "great faith" example and a "little faith" example that sheds light on this degree of difficulty concept. Matthew relates the "great faith" example:

> And when Jesus was entered into Capernaum, there came unto him a centurion, beseeching him, And saying, Lord, my servant lieth at home sick of the palsy, grievously tormented. And Jesus saith unto him, I will come and heal him. The centurion answered and said, Lord, I am not worthy that thou shouldest come under my roof: but speak the word only, and my servant shall be healed. For I am a man under authority, having soldiers under me: and I say to this man, Go, and he goeth; and to another, Come, and he cometh; and to my servant, Do this, and he doeth it. When Jesus heard it, he marvelled, and said to them that followed, Verily I say unto you, I have not found so *great faith*, no, not in Israel. . . . And Jesus said unto the centurion, Go thy way; and as thou hast believed, so be it done unto thee. And his servant was healed in the selfsame hour. (8:5–10, 13)

The centurion's coming to Jesus on behalf of his servant revealed faith. In response Jesus promised, "I will come and heal him." This promise focused on Christ's presence to heal. But then the centurion, knowing he was not a Jew, in humility said, "I am not worthy that thou shouldest come under my roof: but *speak the word only*, and my servant shall be healed. For I am a man [who understands] *authority.*" This statement revealed faith for something greater. The centurion believed not only in Christ's presence to heal, but in His authority to heal from a distance by simply saying "the word only." Jesus responded with "I have not found so *great faith*, no, not in Israel." The centurion's faith was great in the degree of difficulty of what he believed in Christ to do. As a result, Jesus said, "Go your way; and *as thou hast believed*, so be it done unto thee." Immediately the centurion's servant was healed from a distance by the authority of Jesus Christ.

The lesson here is that your faith may be increased in the sense of the degree of difficulty for which you exercise faith. Great faith is great because the aim of the faith is great. Faith is faith. Dependence is dependence. But when the object that faith desires to obtain is great, there is a sense in which the faith may be said to be "great faith."

Matthew 8:23–27 relates the "little faith" example:

And when he was entered into a ship, his disciples followed him. And, behold, there arose a great tempest in the sea, insomuch that the ship was covered with the waves: but he was asleep. And his disciples came to him, and awoke him, saying, Lord, save us: we perish. And he saith unto them, Why are ye fearful, O ye of *little faith*? Then he arose, and rebuked the winds and the sea; and there was a great calm. But the men marvelled, saying, What manner of man is this, that even the winds and the sea obey him!

Christ and His disciples encountered a "great tempest" on the Sea of Galilee causing the boat to be "covered with the waves." But Jesus was "asleep." Then the disciples awoke the Lord saying, "Lord, save us: we perish." This seems to express faith. But Jesus responded, saying, "Why are ye fearful, O ye of *little faith*?" In the parallel passage in Mark, Jesus asked, "How is it that ye have no faith?"(Mark 4:40), and in the parallel passage in Luke, Jesus asked, "Where is your faith?" (Luke 8:25). Evidently, the disciples at that moment had faith for little issues, but not for big issues.

That the disciples came to Jesus with the cry, "Lord, save us" revealed that they had faith in the sense that they came to Jesus. However, they were "fearful" and said, "We perish," revealing that they thought the tempest was too great to overcome. Therefore, they had only "little faith," which is faith for little issues, but in reality they had no faith for greater issues. They needed an increase of faith in the degree of difficulty for which they could trust Christ. In mercy, Jesus blessed their "little faith" in order to increase their faith. The "great tempest" turned into a "great calm" through "little faith." Then the disciples "marvelled, saying, What manner of man is this, that even the winds and the sea obey him!" This enlarged view of Jesus as the object of faith increased their faith in the sense of the degree of difficulty for which they could trust Christ.

Again, the lesson is that your faith may grow in the sense of the degree of difficulty for which you are willing to trust the Lord. Ask the Spirit to enlarge your vision of the Lord Jesus Christ in His authority and power, and your faith will increase. Your faith will grow in the sense of the degree of difficulty for which you are willing to trust God, because you will realize that the Lord possesses all authority and all power and nothing is too difficult for Him.

Acts 14:8–10 relates:

And there sat a certain man at Lystra, impotent in his feet, being a cripple from his mother's womb, who never had walked: The same heard Paul speak: who stedfastly beholding him, and perceiving that he had faith to be healed, Said with a loud voice, Stand upright on thy feet. And he leaped and walked.

The phrase "faith to be healed" describes faith for a great object or simply put, "great faith."

In February of 2010, my sister, Joy Hirth, at the age of 53, experienced the transition of "absent from the body . . . present with the Lord" (2 Cor. 5:6). She had been diagnosed with cancer over eight years before. Most of those years she lived normally, so much so, that others were shocked that she had cancer. But there were several crises along the journey. As each crisis took place, my brother-in-law, Gary, grew from a response of despair (initially) to little faith, and then as faith increased, eventually to great faith. The last crisis, where God granted deliverance, came one year before the Lord saw fit to take Joy home.

The doctors discovered that Joy had a small brain tumor. After a special radiation treatment applied only to that tumor, the doctors discovered three more tumors only three weeks later. This revealed an immediate and great crisis. As Gary sought the Lord, the Spirit led Gary to Mark 2:9, where Jesus said, "Whether is it easier to say to the sick of the palsy, Thy sins be forgiven thee; or to say, Arise, and take up thy bed, and walk?" The Spirit then illumined to Gary's heart that all difficulties to humans are "easy" to God. This conviction, along with several other passages, brought Gary to faith in God for divine healing regarding the recently discovered tumors. The day before he and Joy were to go back to the doctor, Gary testified to the church he pastors in Ann Arbor, Michigan regarding this. The next day two of the tumors could not be found, and the other had not grown! Throughout the next few appointments, the last tumor shrunk to extinction, and the doctors never brought up the tumor issue again. This is a classic example of faith increasing from little faith to great faith in the sense of the degree of difficulty for which faith is exercised.

Duration of Time

A final way faith may be increased is an increase in the duration of time for which faith is exercised. The emphasis here is on the term or duration of time for which faith is exercised on a given issue. This increase of faith is not a matter of size or quantity. If you think that somehow you must muster up more size or quantity of faith itself, then you are back to self-dependence, which is unbelief. You cannot believer harder. Faith is faith. Dependence is dependence. The increase of faith is not in the amount of faith itself. As noted earlier, you may exercise faith for more things. This is an increase in the quantity of occurrences for which faith is exercised. Also, there are some matters that are more difficult to trust God for than other matters. This is an increase in the degree of difficulty for which faith is exercised. But on a given issue of faith, the increase is durative. The only increase is in term, or duration. Thus, faith may be said to be "little" in the sense of being short-termed or "great" in the sense of being long-termed.

Once while teaching this truth to a class, I used the example in the physical realm of sitting on a chair, and I asked the class, "How could you increase your dependence on your chair?" Someone called out, "Gain weight!" But since dependence is dependence, the only real increase would be in how long one sat on their chair. This is an increase of faith in the sense of duration of time.

The New Testament again provides both a negative ("little faith") and positive ("great faith") example in this regard, both of which are again found in Matthew. But there are also several other related passages.

The "little faith" passage is found in Matthew 14:22–33 which relates the story of Jesus walking on water. Matthew's account is the only account that includes Peter also walking on water. Peter's request, "Lord, if it be thou, bid me come unto thee on the water," and Peter's response to the Lord's "Come"—by getting down out of the boat, and the scriptural fact that "he walked on water"—revealed faith indeed. In fact, if you let the weight of the biblical narrative sink in, this was stunning faith. Peter's stepping out of his comfort zone by stepping on to water revealed faith for an extremely difficult matter, humanly speaking. Truly there was great faith regarding the degree of difficulty. "But when he saw the wind boisterous, he was afraid; and beginning to sink [but not sinking], he cried, saying, Lord, save me. And immediately Jesus stretched forth his hand, and caught him, and said unto him, O thou of *little faith*, wherefore didst thou doubt?"

When Peter took his eyes off of Jesus, the object of his faith, and focused on the human sight of the boisterous waves, he stopped trusting Jesus. Jesus' description of Peter's "little faith" emphasized that his faith, though real, was nonetheless short-termed. This nuance is further clarified by Christ's question, "Wherefore didst thou doubt?" Christ questioned Peter as to why he let his faith cease, or come to an end. Had his faith endured or increased in duration, he would not have begun to sink.

The lesson is obvious. Keep your eyes on Jesus to produce enduring faith. The God-ward focus will allow you to navigate through the waves of adversity. Just keep on believing.

Matthew 15:21–28 provides the "great faith" passage by relating the story of the woman of Canaan:

> Then Jesus went thence, and departed into the coasts of Tyre and Sidon. And, behold, a woman of Canaan came out of the same coasts, and cried unto him, saying, Have mercy on me, O Lord, thou son of David; my daughter is grievously vexed with a devil. But he answered her not a word. And his disciples came and besought him, saying, Send her away; for she crieth after us. But he answered and said, I am not sent but unto the lost sheep of the house of Israel. Then came she and worshipped him, saying, Lord, help me. But he answered and said, It is not meet to take the children's bread, and to cast it to dogs. And she said, Truth, Lord: yet the dogs eat of the crumbs which fall from their masters' table. Then Jesus answered and said unto her, O woman, *great is thy faith*: be it unto thee even as thou wilt. And her daughter was made whole from that very hour.

After several seeming rebuffs this Gentile lady, who recognized Jesus as the "Son of David," would not cease to trust in Jesus for deliverance for her demon-possessed daughter. This woman of faith passed several tests of faith, a concept we will address shortly. Her faith endured. Therefore, Jesus exclaimed, "O woman, *great is thy faith*: be it unto thee even as thou wilt," and "her daughter was made whole." Jesus described this lady's faith as "great" because it was long-termed, enduring several obstacles until she received her request.

The lesson here is to keep trusting, to keep enduring in the exercise of faith, even though various obstacles may arise. This allows faith to grow in the sense of the duration of time for which faith is exercised on a given issue. Faith that endures is faith that does not lose heart, as is also illustrated in the case of the widow who kept returning to the unjust judge (Luke 18: 1–8).

The "mustard seed" passages intrigued my interest years ago regarding durative or enduring faith. In Luke 17:5–6 the apostles said to the Lord, "Increase our faith." Jesus responded, "If ye had faith as a grain of mustard seed, ye might say unto this sycamine tree, Be thou plucked up by the root, and be thou planted in the sea; and it should obey you." The wording "had faith" incorporates the imperfect tense, meaning "if you were having faith." The verb tense emphasizes enduring faith. A "mustard seed" referred to one of the smallest of seeds. If "mustard-seed faith" can move a tree, the issue is not quantity or size of faith; the issue is the duration of faith.

In Matthew 17:14–20, the disciples could not cast a particular demon out of a child. Jesus came and cast the demon out. The disciples asked, "Why could not we cast him out?" Jesus responded, "Because of your unbelief: for verily I say unto you, If ye have faith as a grain of mustard seed, ye shall say unto this mountain, Remove hence to yonder place; and it shall remove; and nothing shall be impossible unto you." The wording "have faith" incorporates the present tense meaning, "If you are having faith." Again, the verb tense emphasizes enduring faith. If "mustard-seed faith" can move a mountain, the issue is not quantity or size of faith; the issue is the duration or term of faith.

Later in Matthew 21:21 after the fig tree withered away, Jesus said, "If ye have faith and doubt not . . ." The grammar indicates, "If you are having faith, and do not allow doubt." The emphasis is enduring faith, even through tests that may tempt you to doubt.

This leads us to consider the concept of the testing of your faith. James 1:2 states, "My brethren, count it all joy when ye fall into divers temptations" or various trials. Many wonder, "Why get excited about trials?" James 1:3 answers, "Knowing this, that the trying [testing] of your faith worketh patience." The word "patience" translates from a compound word. The first word in the compound conveys the idea of endurance. The second word in the compound is the noun form of the verb translated "abide" in John 15 and conveys the idea of abiding. The word "abiding" is one of the descriptive New Testament words for faith. Therefore, the compound word means enduring abiding or enduring faith.

Sometimes faith operates in this fashion: The Spirit stirs you with a promise for a particular situation. Being convinced, you embrace that promise by faith. Then everything seems to "go opposite." That is when you need to rejoice. This focus on God in the midst of the testing of faith rejoices the heart of God.

Why rejoice in trials? The answer lies in the fact that the testing of your faith produces enduring faith. The very test of faith reveals that there is faith to test. That should encourage you when you are being tested. Yet God desires that faith to be increased so that even in the face of seemingly impossible obstacles, you keep on trusting in the Lord to remove the mountains of impossibility. This honors and glorifies

God—one of His children has learned to trust Him whatever obstacles sight may offer. Hebrews 10:36 affirms, "For ye have need of patience [enduring dependence], that, after ye have done the will of God, ye might receive the promise."

Personally, I have been slow to learn this lesson of enduring faith that the Lord cultivates through the tests of faith. At times I have "crashed and burned" in a given faith pursuit. But God uses these times of humbling to teach us. Wrong motives and any intrusion of self must be purged. Counterfeit conviction must be distinguished from Holy Spirit conviction. Yet the Lord desires to bring us along if we will follow in faith to the point of staggering not at the promises of God.

My wife and I have traveled in full-time evangelism since 1992. Our home has been in a recreational vehicle since 1995. As I related in the last chapter, in 2002 God graciously gave us a son. Although we travel in revival meetings and conferences over ten months a year, in mid-2005 I began to sense a need to purchase a house. I felt burdened that our son would have a place for special memories. Not getting any younger, I sensed it would be wise to have some type of larger investment. Also, there were tax reasons that encouraged the idea. So for six months I prayed for the Lord's leadership and provision. The burden continued.

Then in January of 2006, while at a conference in Ireland, the Lord guided me to a foundation for faith. I was reading in Proverbs for my morning devotions. At that moment I was not thinking at all of the need for a house. When I read the words "the desire of the righteous shall be granted" (Prov. 10:24), the Lord bore witness with my spirit, "You have your desire. You have the house!" The conviction was deep and real. My heart rejoiced at the promise made real by the Holy Spirit. Then the next day or so when I read "Hope deferred maketh the heart sick: but when the desire cometh, it is a tree of life" (Prov. 13:12), the Lord again communicated, "This too will occur. Your 'desire' will be delayed, but it will come." Then again a few verses later, the Lord spoke through the words, "The desire accomplished is sweet to the soul" (Prov. 13:19). The Lord graciously reinforced to me that on this faith journey, there would be delays, but the "desire" eventually would come.

I thought the delay would be six months to a year. As it turned out, the delay would be four more years! Yet the Spirit's conviction was real and kept me from striving. Every six months, when home for the holidays or a few weeks in the summer, we would search for a house. But God was training me to endure in faith. Nearly two years after the Lord gave me the promise regarding the house, the Lord challenged me afresh with the admonition to "count it all joy" in the trial of faith. Then early in 2008 the Lord stirred me to just thank Him for the house rather than ask for it. When I did this, the Lord granted peace and joy. Without fully understanding the concept at the time, that moment was the essence of the prayer of faith. It was "taking" rather than "asking."

Throughout this entire time the economy declined and real estate prices plummeted downward. The hand of God graciously protected us from purchasing a house before the market fell. By early 2009 my real estate agent said he thought the market was near the bottom, and we ought to search more seriously for a house. During the summer we thought we might have found the right house, but again the "desire" was deferred in the providence of God. This was the biggest disappointment yet, but the Lord reminded us of His word.

Then in the following autumn, one of our meetings in October got rescheduled. I prayed that the Lord would replace it, but the Lord burdened me to go to Michigan. I then sensed that perhaps this was the timing of the Lord for the house. Mortgage rates were low. For three days we searched and searched, but nothing seemed to be the right one. By Wednesday of that week, I was tempted to get discouraged. But in the providence of God, I was scheduled to preach that night at my home church, and the message the Lord laid on my heart was "Faith that Does Not Lose Heart" from Luke 18! By the next day we had made an offer on a house in a beautiful country setting. The offer was accepted. Both housing prices and mortgage rates were as low as they had been in years.

Yet over the next five or six weeks we were still on a roller coaster ride regarding the bank's financing. Hope seemed that it might get deferred yet again. The test of faith continued. But God brought the closing on the house to pass early in December of 2009.

The house God provided sits on a wooded country road near a scenic private lake. It is beautifully suited for adventure for our son and solitude for me, which is a plus for study. The house had been nearly entirely rebuilt in 2005. We purchased the house for the same price as the previous owner did—before he rebuilt it with such beautiful design and materials.

Yet the greatest blessing was not the house. It was the lessons learned on the faith journey taught by the Master Teacher regarding the increase of faith.

Whether speaking of an increase in the quantity of occurrences for which faith is exercised, or an increase in the degree of difficulty for which faith is exercised, or an increase in the duration of time for which faith is exercised, since the Scripture indicates the possibility of a growing faith or a faith that increases, we must join in the heartcry, "Lord, increase our faith."

Appendix

Keswick—A Good Word or a Bad One?

Occasionally I hear people use the label "Keswick" in a derogatory way. Yet others use the term quite positively. Someone who did not know the term would wonder if "Keswick" is a good word or a bad one. The issue, of course, is not the term but what one means by the term.

Historical Background and Theology

Keswick is a beautiful town nestled in the Lake District of England. In 1875 a conference began there which continued annually as The Keswick Convention. Its original stated purpose was for the deepening of spiritual life. To accomplish this purpose a definite theological position was taught—sanctification by faith, sometimes called holiness by faith.

The focus of the theology was on Christ as one's life. This was sometimes called "the Higher Life" or "the Deeper Life" or "the Victorious Life." Although in later years other ideas were attached to some of these labels, their original usage was Christ-focused.

In other words, the "Higher Life," the "Deeper Life," the "Victorious Life," the "Spirit-filled Life," the "Christ-Life" is not a new line of teaching. It is not a mere set of doctrines; it is not a set of motions; it is not a conference, a convention or a movement—it is a Life. That Life is a Person, and His name is Jesus! Jesus is the "Higher Life." Jesus is the "Deeper Life." Jesus is the "Victorious Life." How can it be otherwise? Sanctification or holiness by faith is simply accessing the holy life by faith. It is "I live, yet not I, but Christ liveth in me . . . by faith" (Gal. 2:20). Holiness by faith is accessing the holy life of Jesus to empower holy living and serving. It is becoming "partakers of His holiness" (Heb.12:10), not imitators.

Keswick theology teaches that "progressive sanctification" does not mean an inevitable gradual sanctification, but rather that sanctification is accelerated by faith choices and is hindered by choices of unbelief. Obviously, the Holy Spirit keeps working, but believers are responsible to cooperate in faith for sanctification to progress according to God's will. Keswick teaches that just as justification is by faith, so also sanctification is by faith.

To help people understand how to progress in sanctification, Keswick emphasized a specific theme each of the five days of their convention:

- Sin—sin is the problem: both outer-man sins and especially inner-man sins;

- Provision—Christ is the answer through the cleansing power of His blood and the enabling power of His Spirit;
- Consecration—the access to Christ's provision is through surrender, by yielding to His leadership, and faith, by depending on His enabling;
- The Spirit-filled Life—surrender and faith access Christ's life (the Spirit-filled life for holiness and service);
- Service—the whole point of sanctification by faith is service by faith, primarily by declaring the gospel.

The Keswick Convention began in 1875 and continues to this day. However, as with many movements, eventually the original focus was lost; today the Keswick Convention no longer truly represents its original purpose. The first two generations of Keswick (the first eighty years) held to the original theology—and stayed largely true to its beginning from 1875 through the 1950s. During this time Keswick guarded itself from the extremes of certain factions within the Holiness Movement. However, ecclesiastically, Keswick began to weaken during the Fundamentalist-Modernist controversy of the 1920s and 1930s. Their motto of "All One in Christ" set them up for compromise when this controversy came on the scene. This compromise eventually eroded their theology in significant ways by the 1960s.

First-generation Keswick included as speakers Evan Hopkins (who spoke annually for 39 years), F.B. Meyer (regular speaker from 1887 to 1925), Handley G.C. Moule (regular speaker from the mid-1880s to his death), G. Campbell Morgan, A.T. Pierson, A.J. Gordon, S.D. Gordon, R.A. Torrey, Andrew Murray, Hudson Taylor, Jonathan Goforth and W. H. Griffith Thomas. Second-generation Keswick was led by W. Graham Scroggie, and included Donald Grey Barn-house and J. Oswald Sanders.

Notice how familiar many of these names are and how they are esteemed even to this day. R.A. Torrey was so respected in his day that he was the editor and one of the main authors of the classic apologetic work *The Fundamentals*.[1] A large percentage of the authors used were associated with Keswick theology. This shows that Keswick was mainstream in the beginnings of biblical fundamentalism. Therefore, Keswick was clearly considered orthodox. To denigrate Keswick is to denigrate the roots of fundamentalism.

I prefer to call Keswick theology "revival theology." When one is awakened to the need to access the indwelling life of Christ by faith and begins to appropriate that life for the steps of obedience, personal revival occurs. Revival is a restoration to spiritual life—the life of Christ in you accessed by faith as the animating power to your personality! This doctrine did not begin in 1875 with Keswick. It began in the New Testament (John 10:10, 14–16; Rom. 6–8; 2 Cor. 3:5, 17–18; 9:8; Gal. 2:20; 3:1–5, 14; Eph. 3:17; 5:18; Phil. 1:21; Col. 1:27; 3:4). This is revival theology! In fact, in *The Flaming Tongue*,[2] an account of early twentieth-century revivals which affected at least fifty-seven nations, author J. Edwin Orr repeatedly documents that Keswick-type conferences were used of God to either ignite revival fire or to greatly fuel it.

In the work entitled *Five Views of Sanctification*,[3] J. Robertson McQuilkin wrote the Keswick view, and John Walvoord wrote the Augustinian-Dispensational view. After each author presented his view, he then had opportunity to respond to the other views. McQuilkin said there is no real difference between the Keswick view and the Augustinian-Dispensational view. Also, Walvoord said there was no real difference between the Augustinian-Dispensational view and the Keswick view. Though Keswick deals primarily with sanctification, and dispensational theology is broader than that, essentially Keswick theology is the dispensational theology embraced by many today.

Inaccurate Accusations

Passivity

Some accuse Keswick of passivity. This is probably because Keswick emphasizes resting in Christ. However, the emphasis is not to sit back and do nothing, but rather to trust and obey! The emphasis is not idle passivity but active cooperation—the cooperation of surrendering to the Spirit's leadership and depending on His enabling. This is walking in the Spirit, which obviously involves steps, not quietistic passivity. But the steps are steps of faith, not the mere motions of flesh-dependent activity. This is what brings rest, for when you yoke up with Jesus, He carries the load!

Keswick denounces "struggle theology," which is flesh-dependence in an effort to live the Christian life, because works-sanctification is just as wrong as works-justification (Gal. 3:1–3). You do not get justified by faith and then get sanctified by struggle. Sanctification is also by faith, for "without faith it is impossible to please God" (Heb.11:6). Obviously, there are struggles in life, but flesh-dependence for frustrated Christian living is an unnecessary struggle. Faith for victory means you are depending on the victorious life of Christ to enable you to obey. It is not a matter of you trying to live the Christian life (hollow motions), it is a matter of trusting the indwelling Christ to enable you for the steps of obedience (empowered motions). So victory without trying does not mean victory doing nothing; it means victory with trusting. True faith is not an inward, navel-gazing self-focus; it is focusing rather on Christ, the true object of faith, that He might express His life through yours. To accuse Keswick theology of passivity is simply not accurate.

Subjectivism

Occasionally Keswick theology is labeled derogatorily as being too subjective. This is probably because of Keswick's emphasis on the reality of the Holy Spirit. However, Keswick emphasizes the subjective reality of the Spirit based on the objective boundaries of the Word. The emphasis is by no means the Spirit without the Word. Nor is it the Word without the Spirit. Rather, it is the Word and the Spirit. The Spirit without the Word is delusion, leading to strange fire. The Word without the Spirit is deadness, leading to no fire. But the Word and the Spirit is dynamic, leading to true Holy Spirit fire.

Interestingly, Robert Thomas rightly deals with the dangerous subjectivism of evangelicals in his book called *Evangelical Hermeneutics.*[4] He names many in the evangelical world who are guilty of true subjectivism. But when he seeks to show a right approach, he often quotes J. Robertson McQuilkin as handling matters biblically. (McQuilkin, who wrote several helpful books, is the writer of the Keswick view of sanctification in *Five Views on Sanctification*, which we noted earlier.) Keswick teaches the subjective reality of the Holy Spirit based on the Word, not subjectivism which leaves the scriptural foundation. To accuse Keswick of subjectivism reveals an inaccurate understanding of Keswick teaching.

Second Blessing

Some accuse Keswick of second-blessing theology. But this shows great ignorance of both true second-blessing theology and Keswick theology. Second-blessing theology speaks of receiving a once-for-all second blessing which puts one on a new stage never to fall back to a former stage. Keswick speaks of alternating between two conditions of either walking in the flesh or walking in the Spirit. It is not once for all. Second-blessing theology demands a "second" event. Keswick teaches you were given the whole package at salvation and that you can access the whole blessing immediately (and some do), but that many, because of a lack of understanding, do not until later. Even then it is not a second blessing, but a second, and a third, and a fourth, and so on. Second-blessing theology says that you receive something you did not yet have. Keswick theology teaches that by faith you access your *first* blessing! Some early Keswick writers used the terminology of second blessing (which confuses matters today), but they do so only in the sense that I have described above, which is different from true second-blessing theology.

Sinless Perfectionism

I suppose this charge comes because Keswick theology emphasizes the victorious life of Christ. Obviously, He is perfect. But Keswick makes clear that we still live in the "body of sin" (Rom. 6:6). The focus of Keswick is not that you *cannot* sin, but that you *are able not to* sin because of the indwelling Christ. Keswick makes clear that, tragically Christians sin, but that the focus should not be on being defeated, but rather on victory in Christ by faith. The provision of the indwelling Christ is perfect, but our consistent access of that perfect provision is sadly imperfect. This is quite different from a Wesleyan position. There is no such thing as a Wesleyan/Keswick position. Rather, there is an Augustinian-Dispensational/Keswick position. To accuse Keswick theology of sinless perfectionism is simply not being honest with the facts of Keswick teaching.

Reasons for the Attack

Misinformation

Amazingly, I have been in several settings where speakers had just taught Keswick theology and then said, "Now I'm not talking about Keswick," or, "I'm not talking about the deeper life." This shows that they do not really know what the labels actually mean, but are functioning off of hearsay and concepts which have been attached to the term *Keswick* by the critics of Keswick. First impressions are mind-setting. Someone "bent their ear," or they read the critics of Keswick without actually reading the Keswick authors themselves. Then, when they criticize the term *Keswick*, they are shooting themselves in the foot because they are undermining what they themselves teach. Obviously this is unintentional, but it still is harmful to that which they believe.

Thoroughgoing Calvinism

Not all proclaimed Calvinists clash with Keswick, but those of a thoroughgoing system often do. Keswick emphasizes man's responsibility of faith (sanctification by faith). Some Calvinists claim this is man-centered. But how can God-dependence theology be man-centered? This is a clash between inevitable faith (Calvinism) and responsible faith (Keswick). Does progressive sanctification just inevitably occur for every true child of God, or can it be hindered by unbelief and accelerated by faith? Keswick claims the latter. Interestingly, responsible faith (Keswick) also clashes with the misfocused faith of unfettered choice (Arminianism). Responsible faith means you are responding to the convincing work of the Spirit based on God's Word. It is not unfettered choice, nor is it inevitable. It is a true responsibility.

When I hear or read what some Calvinists claim Keswick teaches, I'm amazed at the inaccuracy. Perhaps some read the critics of Keswick and not Keswick authors themselves. Others may perhaps read Keswick authors but do so with such bias that they do not read what the authors are actually saying. The outcome is major misrepresentation.

Personal Defeat

Some may attack Keswick because they supposedly tried it, and it did not work for them. However, the problem is not with the provision of Christ, but with a misunderstanding of truth or a misapplication of surrender and faith. Some are not truly surrendering (giving up) their sin; they just don't like their guilt. Some may have misunderstandings regarding faith, what it is and how it works. If you have a besetting sin or are ineffective in service, it is always easier to blame something other than your own responsible choices.

Satanic Attack

Satan attacks revival truth! He is the master deceiver. Revival theology (Keswick) threatens his turf. Much of the controversy is stirred up by his deceptions. When you understand that Keswick-type conferences were used to ignite revival fires or fuel them in the early twentieth-century revivals, it is no wonder that Satan has attacked Keswick theology in order to prevent another great wave of revival blessing.

Conclusion

Obviously, an article which is brief in its nature cannot deal with all the details of the present confusion around the word *Keswick*. May I suggest that you read the Keswick authors themselves? Here are a few to consider:

- G. Campbell Morgan, *The Spirit of God* (Eugene, OR: Wipf and Stock, 2003).
- Evan Hopkins, *The Law of Liberty in the Spiritual Life* (Fort Washington, PA: CLC Publications, 1991).
- J. Elder Cummings, *Through the Eternal Spirit* (Minneapolis: Bethany Fellowship, 1965).
- Handley G.C. Moule, *Practicing the Promises* (Chicago: Moody Press, 1975).

I would also suggest reading Moule's treatment of Romans 6–8 in his commentary on Romans,[5] F. B. Meyer's many books, A. J. Gordon's writings, A. T. Pierson's works, and so forth. Steven Barabas quotes from many Keswick authors in his book entitled *So Great Salvation: The History and Message of the Keswick Convention*.[6]

So is Keswick a good word or a bad one? If you mean sanctification by faith thus accessing the victorious life of Christ, that is gloriously good! However, I prefer to use the label "revival theology." The issue, of course, is not a label, but truth.

Jesus Christ is the only one who can live the Christian life! Jesus is the Christian life. But He lives in you so that you, yet not you, but Christ in you can live the Christian life! When you got saved, Christ moved in—to live His life, not yours! But this is not automatic. As you received Christ by faith, you also must walk by faith one step at a time (Col. 2:6). This is accessing the eternal life as the abundant life. This is sanctification by faith. Ultimately, this is revival reality.

For those of us who believe the theology of Christ in you, accessed by faith, the derogatory slurs against this truth are not small matters. Jesus *is* the Victorious Life, the Higher Life, the Deeper Life, the Spirit-filled Life, the Revived Life, the Hidden Life—the Christ-Life! To us, when holiness by faith—the holy life accessed by faith—is attacked, the attack is ultimately on the indwelling life of Christ.

Endnotes

Chapter 3

1. Jessie Penn-Lewis, *The Conquest of Canaan* (Fort Washington, PA: CLC Publications, 1989, 1992), 9.
2. Rebecca English, *Living the Christ Life* (Fort Washington, PA: CLC Publications), 279–80.
3. William Newell, *Romans Verse by Verse* (Chicago: Moody, 1948), 213.
4. Charles Trumbull, *Victory in Christ* (Fort Washington, PA: CLC Publications, 2007), 92.
5. Ibid., 87–88.
6. Ruth Paxson, *The Wealth, Walk and Warfare of the Christian* (New York: Fleming H. Revell, 1939), 58.

Chapter 5

1. S. D. Gordon, *Quiet Talks on Prayer* (New York: Fleming H. Revell Company, n.d.), 62–63.

Chapter 6

1. Ruth Stewart, *James Stewart Missionary* (Asheville, NC: Gospel Projects, Inc., 1977), 237.

2. James O. Fraser, *The Prayer of Faith* (Littleton, CO: OMF International, 1958, 2008), 19–21.

Chapter 7

1. Fritz Rienecker and Cleon Rogers, *Linguistic Key to the Greek New Testament* (Grand Rapids: Zondervan, 1980), 191.
2. Ibid., 488.
3. Wigram-Green, *The New Englishman's Greek Concordance and Lexicon* (Peabody, MA: Hendrickson Publishers, Inc., 1982), 885.
4. William E. Arndt and F. Wilbur Gingrich, *A Greek-English Lexicon of the New Testament and Other Early Christian Literature*, Second Edition (Chicago: University of Chicago Press, 1979), 563.

Appendix

1. *The Fundamentals: A Testimony to the Truth*, edited by A.C. Dixon and later by R.A. Torrey, is a set of ninety essays in twelve volumes published from 1910 to 1915 by the Bible Institute of Los Angeles. Designed to affirm the fundamentals of Christian faith and defend against heretical beliefs, they are widely considered to be the foundation of the modern fundamentalist movement.
2. J. Edwin Orr, *The Flaming Tongue* (Chicago: Moody Press, 1973).
3. Melvin E. Dieter, et al., *Five Views on Sanctification* (Grand Rapids: Zondervan, 1987).
4. Robert Thomas, *Evangelical Hermeneutics* (Grand Rapids: Kregel, 2002).

5. Handley G.C. Moule, *The Epistle to the Romans* (Fort Washington, PA: CLC Publications, 2001).

6. Steven Barabas, *So Great Salvation: The History and Message of the Keswick Convention* (Eugene, OR: Wipf and Stock, 2005).

Bibliography

Arndt, William F. and F. Wilbur Gingrich. *A Greek-English Lexicon of the New Testament and Other Early Christian Literature.* Chicago: University of Chicago Press, 1979.

English, Rebecca. *Living the Christ Life.* Fort Washington, PA: CLC Publications, 2009.

Fraser, James O. *The Prayer of Faith.* Littleton, CO: OMF International, 1958, 2008.

Gordon, S.D. *Quiet Talks on Prayer.* New York: Fleming H. Revell Company, n.d.

Newell, William. *Romans Verse by Verse.* Chicago: Moody Press, 1948.

Paxson, Ruth. *The Wealth, Walk and Warfare of the Christian.* New York: Fleming H. Revell Company, 1939.

Penn-Lewis, Jessie. *The Conquest of Canaan.* Fort Washington, PA: CLC Publications, 1989.

Rienecker, Fritz and Cleon Rogers. *Linguistic Key to the Greek New Testament*. Grand Rapids: Zondervan, 1980.

Stewart, Ruth. *James Stewart, Missionary*. Asheville, NC: Gospel Projects, Inc., 1977.

Trumbull, Charles. *Victory in Christ*. Fort Washington, PA: CLC Publications, 2007.

Wigram-Green. *The New Englishman's Greek Concordance and Lexicon*. Peabody, MA: Hendrikson Publishers, Inc., 1982.

READ THE REMARKABLE STORY OF
the founding of
CLC INTERNATIONAL

Leap of Faith

"Any who doubt that Elijah's God still lives ought to read of the money supplied when needed, the stores and houses provided, and the appearance of personnel in answer to prayer." —Moody Monthly

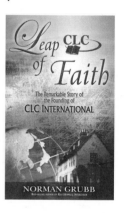

Is it possible that the printing press, the editor's desk, the Christian bookstore and the mail order department can glow with the fast-moving drama of an "Acts of the Apostles"?

Find the answer as you are carried from two people in an upstairs bookroom to a worldwide chain of Christian bookcenters multiplied by nothing but a "shoestring" of faith and by committed, though unlikely, lives.

This book was produced by CLC Publications. We hope it has been life-changing and has given you a fresh experience of God through the work of the Holy Spirit. CLC Publications is an outreach of CLC Ministries International, a global literature mission with work in over fifty countries. If you would like to know more about us or are interested in opportunities to serve with a faith mission, we invite you to contact us at:

CLC Ministries International
PO Box 1449
Fort Washington, PA 19034

Phone: 215-542-1242
E-mail: orders@clcpublications.com
Website: www.clcpublications.com

DO YOU LOVE GOOD CHRISTIAN BOOKS?
Do you have a heart for worldwide missions?

You can receive a FREE subscription to
CLC's newsletter on global literature missions
Order by e-mail at:

clcworld@clcusa.org
Or fill in the coupon below and mail to:

**PO Box 1449
Fort Washington, PA 19034**

FREE *CLC WORLD* SUBSCRIPTION!

Name: _____

Address:_____

_____

Phone: _____ E-mail:_____

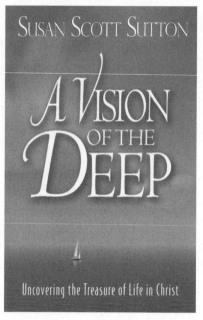

A VISION OF THE DEEP

Susan Scott Sutton

Uncovering the Treasure of Life in Christ

Has your walk with Christ become
a duty rather than a passion?

Susan Sutton takes us beyond a sense of obligation and
responsibility in the Christian life to give us a "vision of the
deep." If you are dissatisfied with "surface living," join Susan in
this life-altering venture to lose yourself in the fathomless depths
of Jesus Christ.

ISBN 13: 978-0-87508-786-3

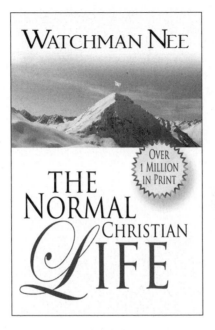

THE NORMAL CHRISTIAN LIFE

Watchman Nee

The Normal Christian Life is Watchman Nee's great Christian classic unfolding the central theme of "Christ Our Life." Nee reveals the secret of spiritual strength and vitality that should be the normal experience of every Christian.

Starting from certain key passages in Romans, he defines clearly and vividly the essential steps in the personal faith and walk of the believer. His emphasis on the cross and resurrection of Jesus Christ contains fresh spiritual insights that have proven a blessing to many.

ISBN: 978-0-87508-990-4

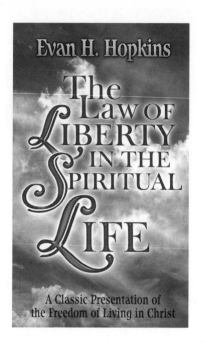

THE LAW OF LIBERTY IN THE SPIRITUAL LIFE

Evan H. Hopkins

"Freedom is an essential characteristic of the life of fellowship with Christ." Evan Hopkins writes. "Christ not only imparts life, He also provides that which is necessary for its emancipation."

One of the earliest speakers at the famous Keswick Conventions of the late 19th and early 20th centuries in England, Hopkins shares the secret of true Christian liberty: the miraculous truth of living "in Christ." This is a book for those longing for a deeper, more intimate knowledge of the great grace of God.

ISBN: 978-0-87508-273-8

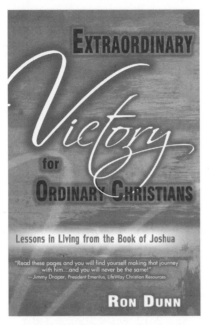

EXTRAORDINARY VICTORY
FOR ORDINARY CHRISTIANS

Ron Dunn

The Christian Life is a victorious life . . . and anything less is a cheap imitation of the real thing.

Don't be resigned to mediocrity

Drawing on the book of Joshua, "God's object lesson on victorious living," Ron Dunn presents the great news that God wants every Christian to experience the life of victory. "While the Bible admits defeat, it never assumes it," Ron says. "The predominant theme throughout Scripture is victory, and anyone living less than victoriously is falling short of the divine intention. Too many Christians are struggling to win a victory that Jesus already won on the cross—2,000 years ago!"

ISBN: 978-1-936143-16-0